MW01630887

# *Rave Reviews* for The Humor Advantage

"Michael hits the nail on the head when it comes to the balance of fun and professionalism. His book is full of brilliant real world examples of ways to utilize humor and improve company culture. It has my brain swirling with new ideas we can bring to Men In Kilts."

**– Nicholas Brand, Founder, Men In Kilts Window Cleaning**

"This book could revolutionize my culture. You pull information, quotes and case studies from all areas of business and at all levels. It takes any business on a fun ride to get their workplace to a happy place with super engaged people and a culture of belonging. I can't wait for my executives to read this; they'll have a new set of eyes to see what you can actually do in a business to get serious work done with a fun, positive attitude. This is a fire hose of information and value for anyone trying to turn their culture upside down! You nailed it!"

**– Michael Easton, President and CEO Argus Industries**

"Wow! Eureka! Light bulbs popping in my brain! The Humor Advantage gives entrepreneurs a barrel-full of creative ideas to accelerate their sales growth while making your business a destination for great employees and ecstatic customers."

**Jon Schallert, founder, DestinationUniversity.com**

"The business world has been waiting for this book: Hundreds of insights and specific examples of how you can create humor, deliver humor and profit from humor in your business. 'Funny' rhymes with 'money' for a reason. Michael gets it ... and now you will too."

**– Donald Cooper, MBA, Business speaker**

"Michael Kerr is a very funny guy, but in his new book he provides some seriously important ideas about using humor in the workplace. In his normal witty style, he teaches practical ideas and gives you the inspiration to use them to better your business, your profits and your personal life."

**– Mark Sanborn,**
**author of *The Fred Factor***

"This book is your strategic plan for creating an exceptionally inspiring workplace—do yourself a favor and buy one copy for yourself and another for your boss!"

**– James Robbins,**
**author of *Nine Minutes on Monday***

"As Michael Kerr says in *The Humor Advantage,* humor and success in business isn't a 'chicken or egg' thing - it's both. Success in business helps create upbeat employees and having upbeat employees helps create a successful business. Take your business up a notch—read this book!"

**– Joe Calloway, author of**
***Be the Best at What Matters Most***

"Leveraging *The Humor Advantage* in your business will drive outrageous results that will help you laugh all the way to the bank. A must-read for any business that wants to attract and keep top talent, engage employees, boost sales and turn customers into passionate, lifelong fans!"

**– Colleen Francis, sales expert**
**and author of *Nonstop Sales Boom***

# THE Humor ADVANTAGE

Why Some Businesses Are
LAUGHING All The Way To The Bank

Michael Kerr

Bulk purchases of this book are available to corporations, institutions and other organizations. For bulk order rates contact info@mikekerr.com, phone 403-609-2640 or visit our website at www.thehumoradvantage.com

Front and back cover design: Kelly Stauffer, Kelly Stauffer Graphics
Interior page design: Articulate Eye Design, Saskatoon, SK
Indexing: Anne Peterson

Printed in Canada

Library and Archives Canada Cataloguing in Publication

Kerr, Michael, 1962-

The Humor Advantage: Why Some Businesses are Laughing All the Way to the Bank/Michael Kerr.

ISBN 978-0-9688461-2-4

# Table of Contents

# Foreword

"The number one premise of business is that it need not be boring or dull. It ought to be fun. If it's not fun, you're wasting your life."
– Tom Peters

When it came to leveraging the humor advantage to help brand a business, I knew there was one person I needed to talk to: Mr. Brand. (I mean, seriously, who else could it *possibly* have been?)

Although the company Nicholas Brand so successfully branded uses the cheeky tagline, 'No peeking,' he was kind enough to offer me a glance under his kilt, so to speak. The company that Brand founded, you see, was the highly successful window washing business, Men In Kilts.

Ready to launch his solo endeavor in 2002, Brand knew he needed a name and a hook… something, *anything,* that would help him stand out from his competitors. After seeing a report on the evening news of a window washer dressed like Spiderman (we'll return to window-washing superheroes later), one of Brand's friends suggested he wear a kilt at work, to pay homage to his Scottish ancestry. A self-described introvert, the scheme sounded a bit disconcerting to Brand, to say the least. Sure, he was looking for exposure, but that's not what he had in mind!

But Brand agreed that wearing a kilt would definitely make him memorable. So after his wife hand-sewed him one (which now hangs in his office), all he needed was a name to accompany the unconventional look. After tossing about various Scottish-sounding generic names, he landed upon Men In Kilts, drawing inspiration from the blockbuster movie, *Men In Black.*

Brand's brand was well received from the start, but it exploded to dizzying heights once he traded his rusting Honda Accord for a van featuring the image of a kilt-wearing window washer. The playful branding caught the eye of the media, and before long Men In Kilts was being featured in magazines, newspapers and on television. Men In Kilts is now a thriving and rapidly growing franchise business, with locations throughout North America.

It's easy to dismiss Men In Kilts as just another story about gimmicky marketing. Yes, the humorous brand helped them attract untold amounts of free publicity. But as Brand points out, "The word 'gimmick' can have a bad connotation. But it shouldn't! It's really about standing out from the crowd. It's about what makes you different than your competitors."

And it really would be a mere gimmick if there was nothing under the kilt. Fortunately for its customers, Men In Kilts has a stated policy that their employees must wear something under *there* at all times. Metaphorically speaking, Brand also understands that the best branding in the world won't sustain success unless there's a highly professional, service-oriented business behind it all.

"Yes, we take ourselves lightly and have a lot of fun, but we take our business and our customers' needs seriously. We want to earn the reputation as being the #1 window-washing company in the world, but we want to make it fun for us and our customers at the same time. It's not a choice between fun and professionalism for us, it's about choosing to have both."

The fun brand has helped them attract more than free media attention. They've also attracted employees who don't take themselves too seriously (they'll be climbing ladders wearing a kilt, after all). In fact, Brand has found that the kilts act as a built-in hiring filter, screening out potential fun-suckers. Even better: The brand attracts customers who are easy to work with and want to have a bit of fun as well.

Men In Kilts is just one of hundreds of success stories that demonstrate that work doesn't always resemble a Dilbert cartoon and yes, it really *is* possible to laugh all the way to the bank.

But before we dive into more of those outrageous success stories from around the globe, let's get real for a moment: Work can, at times, be a real drag.

There, I said it. Feel better?

Yes, the humor advantage is all about the power of having more fun at work and purposefully using humor to help you, your team and your business succeed—maybe even to laugh all the way to the bank. But, let's not sugarcoat things. There's a reason it's called work and a reason you get a paycheck—it's not always a barrel of laughs.

Work can be difficult, insanely challenging, or—at times—maddeningly boring.

Work can be mentally and physically draining.

Work can be full of petty politics, pain-in-the-posterior co-workers and meetings about meetings where, as *Star Trek's* Captain Kirk once wryly observed, "Minutes are taken and hours wasted."

And don't forget what got you there in the first place: Yes, that confounding daily ritual known as The Commute. Have you *seen* the way some people drive? As George Carlin once observed, everyone who drives slower than you is an idiot and everyone who drives faster is a maniac. Chances are you've pumped out more stress hormones during your morning commute than a three-legged gazelle at a watering hole... and you haven't even *started* work yet!

Then there are *The Customers*. You know the ones....

The high-maintenance ones.

The ones who breathe heavily and smell like cheese.

The ones who won't leave you alone... and the ones you don't want to be alone with.

Fortunately, back at the office you can escape The Customers and immerse yourself in fun stuff like mergers and downsizings and rightsizings and change initiatives that never change and reorganizations that never seem to end up with anything remotely organized so why do they keep calling it a reorganization when it didn't seem to be very organized to begin with?

And don't get me started on PowerPoint presentations that seem to be neither powerful nor make a point.

Finally (you may have noticed), work is just a *wee* bit of a time sucker. For many of us, 70% of our waking hours are spent at work. I hate to be the bearer of bad news, but there's a very good chance you'll spend more time with your boss and co-workers than with your own family.

Add this all together and it's not particularly surprising to learn that, according to a 2013 Gallup poll, only 13% of employees worldwide are fully engaged in their jobs.[1] *Ouch.*

So work is a soul-sucking, fun-sucking, Dilbert-like experience. Scratch that. Work is a soul-sucking, fun-sucking, Dilbert-like experience... for *some* people.

Fortunately, as you'll soon discover, there *are* islands of hope out there, islands you don't want to be voted off of even on days when you feel like you're in survivor mode. These workplaces are thriving, even laughing all the way to the bank. Why? Because they've tapped into the humor advantage.

The great news is that *anyone,* whether at the individual, team, or corporate level, can learn how to tap into their own version of the humor advantage.

## WHY *THE HUMOR ADVANTAGE?*

This book had its genesis more than eighteen years ago, after I voted myself off my own island, a dysfunctional workplace I originally thought was Utopia. Okay, so maybe not quite Utopia. But for several years, I truly loved my job. I looked forward to coming to work every Monday morning. I worked with a great group of people. We worked hard and we had fun doing it.

As a manager, I practiced a healthy dose of humor as often as I could. My sense of humor was a life raft whenever the seas of organizational life got too choppy. And because of our collective sense of humor, we communicated better, performed better as a team and were more creative.

Then, as I hear from so many of my clients, the organization lost its, well, *mojo.* People quit having fun. Employees lost their sense of humor. Like the proverbial canary in the coal mine, the *absence* of humor in the workplace was the first sign that the organization was headed for troubled waters. It was time to vote myself off the island.

So now, as a recovering manager who witnessed first-hand the highs and lows of the professional world, I've dedicated my career to seeking out, writing about and speaking about leaders, workplaces and businesses that dare to be different, that dare to have fun and put people and humanity *first.*

*The Humor Advantage* is about the intersection between play and purpose, seriousness and silliness, business and fun. It's about how a healthy sense of humor, passion and fun can help your organization drive outrageous results.

Is *The Humor Advantage* a magic elixir that will instantly transform your workplace? Of course not. This is *not* a travel guide to Utopia Inc., where employees clasp hands and belt out *We Are The World* every Monday morning while puppies and unicorns frolic under rainbows. But it's my sincere hope that this book will challenge your conventional thinking about work and inspire you to change some (or perhaps lots) of the ways you do things in your business.

If the stories, tips, ideas and inspiration in *The Humor Advantage* don't help you laugh all the way to the bank, then ask yourself one simple question: All things being equal, would you rather have the same level of success you currently have but with a little more fun thrown into the mix, or the same level of success but with *less* fun?

After all, no one on their death bed ever said, "Boy... if I had to do it all over again I'd have less fun, take myself more seriously and work in a more stressful workplace." It seems like an obvious choice to me. As Mike Argus, CEO of Argus Industries, told me, "Work is hard enough as it is without making it any harder!"

That being said, I hope you have as much fun reading *The Humor Advantage* as I had writing it.

# 1

# Getting Up to Some Funny Business—*You Can't Be Serious?*

"Businesses have a misguided sense that work and play are opposites."

— Tom Kelly, Cofounder of IDEO

Humor in the workplace is the Rodney Dangerfield of human resources management. Like the late, tie-tugging comedian, the topic doesn't get much respect. After all, humor as a competitive advantage isn't taught in most MBA programs.

Clown school? Possibly.

Community college improv course? You betcha.

But business school? Not so much.

Because of the nature of humor and its seemingly diametric opposition to loftier pursuits such as seriousness, hard work and, well, making money, humor gets easily dismissed as a trivial topic. Yet more and more businesses are demonstrating a tangible humor advantage that is helping them laugh all the way to the bank. And employees and managers are taking advantage of their sense of humor to help them be more successful in their careers.

Let's start our journey by defining what appropriate workplace humor is, lest you worry that you'll soon be prancing around the office in a pair of floppy clown shoes. Having a sense of humor in the workplace is *not* about telling jokes, being a stand-up comedian, or being the office clown. It's not about being an extrovert or practicing fake enthusiasm. It's not even always about being funny (I can already hear you sighing with relief).

Having a sense of humor is about adopting a spirit of playfulness and fun. It's about appreciating the incongruous events and absurd moments that flitter by us every day. It's about embracing a sense of balance, a sense of perspective and a sense of humanity. Like our other senses, humor is a way of interpreting and filtering the events in the world around us.

Let me be clear: I am not advocating being *un*professional in any way, shape, or form. In fact, the desire for professionalism in most workplaces is so important that we may need to rethink exactly what it means to "be professional."

Too often the desire to "be professional" is used as an excuse to downplay or even banish any semblance of fun and humor at work. "Acting professional" becomes synonymous with being earnest, acting solemn, playing it safe, or leaving one's personality at home. Acting professional can even become code for championing style over substance: It doesn't matter what you actually do, so long as you *look* and *sound* professional.

But there's nothing remotely professional about acting like an automaton. Isn't it ironic, after all, that the *more* seriously people take themselves (presumably with a goal of being taken seriously) the *less* seriously other people actually take them?

What I'm advocating is simply the need to laugh at ourselves more, to take ourselves *less* seriously in order to be *more* effective and (dare I say?) even *more* professional at work.

The American philosopher John Dewey once observed, "To be playful and serious at the same time is possible and it defines the ideal mental condition." *That's* the essence of humor that needs to be embraced—not feared—at the highest levels of management.

Having a sense of humor is also about being authentic. After all, rarely are we more real than when we laugh. We are never more human than when humor shatters the professional masks we sometimes wear, revealing the true human being lurking beneath the corporate façade. This is likely why studies show a positive correlation between humor and trust: We tend to trust people more when we sense they are the real deal and humor helps us appear more vulnerable and genuine.

As you'll see, humor is a comfort, a catalyst and a connector that *any* front-line employee, sales rep, leader, or (gasp!) even CEO can include in their toolkit to improve results. And it's a powerfully effective way to inject some life into your brand that will help your business stand out from the herd, to be heard like never before.

## THE RUBBER-CHICKEN-AND-EGG RELATIONSHIP OF HUMOR AT WORK

Does humor help create a better workplace environment where people whistle while they work, or does it merely reflect a positive workplace culture?

Paul Spiegelman, CEO of The Beryl Companies, told me how he's blunt with his employees about the need for them to bring a good attitude along for the ride.[1] It's a basic expectation of his and why Beryl, as you'll discover, is so diligent about its hiring practices. Like so many successful companies, Beryl recognizes that one of the keys to creating a great culture is hiring people with the right attitude, *then* training them for the rest of their duties.

Attitude, without question, is important. But it's only half the equation. It's very easy for a leader or cheesy motivational speaker to implore you to fire up your attitude and turn your frown upside down because—gee whiz, kids—it takes forty-three muscles to frown but only seventeen to smile!

If only it were that simple.

(For starters, plastic surgeon Dr. David H. Song of the University of Chicago Medical Center says that frowning requires only eleven muscles while smiling requires twelve.[2] So take that, smile-pushers!)

The challenge goes beyond mere anatomy. Even in a positive, family-friendly, fun workplace such as Beryl, Spiegelman recognizes that asking people to have a good attitude is only the beginning: "The leadership team and the company itself also need to do their part. The onus is on us to create the kind of workplace environment that makes it easy for everyone to bring a good sense of humor and a positive attitude into work each and every day."

That's why it's helpful to think of humor as both the chicken *and* the egg. (Or, perhaps, the *rubber* chicken and the egg?)

By that I mean exactly what Spiegelman stresses. A sense of humor really *can* help you do your job better and help you grow your business. But a great attitude and healthy sense of humor also *reflects* success; it's a byproduct of doing the right things at work to build an inspiring workplace culture where you make it easy for yourself, your employees and your customers to embrace a healthy sense of humor. As Dilbert creator Scott Adams said, "Humor in the workplace comes naturally *after* you've done everything right."

## BUT SERIOUSLY, CAN PUNCH LINES MAKE A DIFFERENCE TO YOUR BOTTOM LINE?

"Did you hear the one about the manager who got a bigger bonus because she had a great sense of humor?"

You probably haven't heard this one making the rounds at the water cooler, because it's not a joke. It's actually one of several findings from a study by Fabio Sala, a consultant with the Hay Group's McClelland Center for Research and Innovation.[3] Sala found a positive correlation between the size of managers' bonuses and their use of humor. The study also found that outstanding executives use humor more than *twice* as often as the so-called average executives. Studies like this point to a growing consensus that if you are serious about your career, sometimes it pays to *not* be serious... at least, not *too* serious.

This may explain why some businesses even hire for a sense of humor and why—if you're in the job market—you may want to hone your ha-ha. A survey of 737 CEOs by Hodge-Cronin and Associates found that a whopping 98% of CEOs would rather hire someone with a good sense of humor than someone with a more serious demeanor.[4] What's more, 91% of executives in a Robert Half International survey agreed that humor is important for career advancement, while 84% believed people with a good sense of humor do a better job than their counterparts who flex their funny bone less often.[5]

A study in 2007 by Chris Robert, an assistant professor at the University of Missouri, found that employees with a good sense of humor showed higher levels of productivity, communicated more effectively and were psychologically more connected to their organization; while leaders with a good sense of humor were more effective at motivating employees, communicating and reducing workplace stress.[6]

Even NASA has stated that one of the personality traits it looks for in future astronauts is humor, believing that such candidates are more flexible, creative and better able to deal with stress. (Of course, if you're flying to Mars for seven months with only one other crew member to keep you company, you better have a good sense of humor!)

Once your foot is in the door (or aboard a Mars-bound spaceship, as the case may be), evidence shows that a well-flexed funny bone can also help you maintain a thriving career. Humor is an important social lubricant, bonding tool and trust builder. A healthy sense of humor is also one of the most effective stress busters available and helps people distance themselves from workplace tension, maintain a more balanced perspective and overcome obstacles. Moreover, humor is one of the best catalysts for creative thinking, which makes sense, given that humor and creativity are about combining unrelated ideas and looking at something in a different light.

But it's not just downward-gazing leaders who are drawn to those with a sense of humor. Employees also want to be led by bosses who know how to walk through life with a bit of levity in their step. A survey by the Bell Leadership Institute asked more than 2,700 employees to describe the strengths of their leaders.[7] They found that by far the two most frequently used phrases were "a strong work ethic" and "sense of humor." The study found that leaders who were seen as working hard but still having fun had a strong edge over their more staid counterparts. Even at a very conservative organization such as the United States Military Academy at West Point, students rated 'good' leaders significantly more humorous than 'bad' ones.[8]

So what is it about humor that makes people better leaders? One of the reasons is the close relationship between humor and trust. Professor William Hampes from Illinois' Black Hawk College studied this tie and discovered that, like Sheldon and Amy from the *Big Bang Theory*, it is, indeed, a rather unconventional match made in heaven. His research revealed that the people who were considered the most trustworthy had the greatest appreciation of humor, used humor as a coping tool and used humor in social situations.[9]

(On an intriguing side note, particularly as a male with a great sense of humor, a study reported in *Psychology Today* found that women think humor-generating men are hot, "...because wit signals intelligence and creativity."[10])

So it would appear that nurturing a healthy sense of humor at work might just help land you that new job, score that bonus, thrive in your career and help you be seen as a more credible, trustworthy leader.

But what about your company's bottom line? Well, don't take my word for it. In *The Humor Advantage* we'll tell the stories of countless companies that have all experienced tremendous results by effectively putting humor to work. These companies run the gamut of industry and geography and include such names as:

- Kulula Airlines in South Africa, whose fun—and occasionally downright hilarious—marketing efforts have helped brand them as the funniest airline in the world and taken it to phenomenal heights;
- Online shoe business Zappos, which has built a dynamic culture that attracts huge waiting lists of potential employees;
- AFA JCDecaux, a Danish outdoor advertising company that credits its use of humor as a major factor in increasing sales, improving customer service and lowering employee turnover rates.

Now for a word of caution: Don't for a moment get sucked into thinking that *your* workplace or *your* business is somehow different than everybody else's and that humor couldn't possibly work for you. It doesn't matter if you're blue collar or white collar, small or large, running an airline or even (as we'll see), commanding a ship in the US Navy—humor can have a profound impact on your organization's much-coveted bottom line.

In fact, a Hewitt and Associates study found that organizations with higher levels of employee engagement (humor is by no means the only factor here, but it *can* play a significant role in boosting engagement levels) outperformed other companies on the stock market, showing increased shareholder returns of 19% relative to companies with less-engaged employees.[11] A Wharton School of Business study also found that businesses with the happiest employees performed notably better financially than those with a less-happy staff.[12] Gretchen Rubin in the book *The Happiness Project* details how happier employees tend to come up with more ideas, create better-performing teams, set loftier goals and are viewed as being friendlier.[13]

Finally, the Great Places to Work Institute found that in Fortune 100 companies officially recognized as great places to work, 81% of employees agreed with the statement: "I work in a fun working environment." In companies rated as merely "*good* places to work," only 62% agreed that they work in a fun environment.[14]

The success equation then, it would appear, for many businesses is: More Funny = More Money.

So let's find out how businesses are delivering better results through humor and in the process, laughing all the way to the bank.

### Key Messages

1. A sense of humor isn't about being funny, telling jokes or being an extrovert. It's about a sense of perspective, a sense of balance and a sense of humanity. It's about taking yourself lightly in order to take your work seriously.

2. A healthy sense of humor can help you achieve greater results at an individual, team and organizational level. It truly can help you laugh all the way to the bank.

# 2

# Humor as a Brand Advantage—*If You Build It Right, They Will Come*

> "What we are looking for, first and foremost, is a sense of humor. We hire attitudes."
>
> — Herb Kelleher, cofounder and former CEO of Southwest Airlines

The energy at the corporate headquarters of Zappos—an online shoe and clothing retailer based in Las Vegas, Nevada—was infectious. Festooned with balloons, off-the-wall decorations, outrageously funny posters and colorful streamers, the office looked like a Mardi Gras parade had just blown into town. Employees seemed genuinely excited about returning to work... even on a Monday morning. This was *not* your typical Dilbertesque office.

As I chatted with the ebullient and charming "Director of First Impressions" (the job titles at Zappos are not only fun and creative, they reflect the true focus of the work) I noticed a delivery man watching the scene of exuberant employees arriving to work, studying them the way I imagine Jane Goodall might watch over a newly discovered troop of chimpanzees. After about three minutes of loitering about the reception area, the courier leaned over the front counter and finally popped the question: "Do you have any job openings?"

When the delivery guy asks if there are any job openings in your business, chances are you're doing a few things right.

## BUILDING YOUR OWN FIELD OF DREAMS

Your workplace culture is all about *how* you do the things you do. It's your DNA. It's a combination of the written and unwritten rules in your company. It's what the veterans tell the new kids what they need to do to survive. It's about answering challenging questions such as, "Would you recommend your workplace to your best friend or a family member as a great place to work?" and "Does your workplace live up to the hype in your help-wanted ads?"

Every organization has a culture. But great cultures don't happen by accident. You can't buy your culture at Costco (chances are it'd be too big anyway) or Ikea (you'd probably have parts left over that even your IT department wouldn't know what to do with). You can't fake a great culture... although judging by a cursory scan of many help-wanted ads, a lot of companies try.

To build a truly inspiring culture you need to be *intentional*. In fact, the Human Capital Institute (a leading talent management agency) recommends that 70% of a leader's time be spent on talent management and nurturing the culture.[1] In other words: Fostering a strong culture *is the job of a leader.*

Which is exactly why Zappos has made Fortune's list of "Best Companies to Work For" five years and running—climbing all the way to the sixth slot in 2011. CEO Tony Hsieh and fellow executives set two long-term goals back in 2002, only three years after their founding: 1) achieve more than one billion dollars in sales and 2) make the cut on Fortune's much-coveted list.

Check... and check. Mission more than accomplished.

Zappos (a variation of "zapatos" the Spanish word for "shoes") is the largest online shoe retailer on earth, achieving over a billion dollars in annual sales. The phenomenal growth and success of the company has been achieved through its outrageous commitment to customer service (more on that later) and a relentless focus on building a dynamic, fun culture as reflected through at least half of its ten core values:

Value #1: Deliver WOW Through Service
Value #3: Create Fun and a Little Weirdness
Value #4: Be Adventurous, Creative and Open-Minded
Value #7: Build a Positive Team and Family Spirit
Value #9: Be Passionate and Determined

Don't for a moment think that these are merely empty platitudes or feel-good slogans. After spending a few days at Zappos HQ, I was convinced this was a culture like few others on the planet. Indeed, their *Culture Book*—an annual tradition in which employees describe the company's culture in their own words—recounts countless examples of how these values are brought to life and treated as real commitments to employees and customers.

So just how "fun and a little weird" (value #3) can Zappos get? Well, they have an annual "Bald and Blue Day" where employees are invited to shave their heads, paint their hair blue, or wear temporary tattoos. They've held events where employees raised money for charity by throwing whipped cream pies at the senior executives and they've brought in a petting zoo for employees.

Zappos's Insights "Culture Evangelist," Jon Wolske, points out that it's not just the fun physical environment, games room, great food, wacky events and team-building experiences that create their exceptional culture.[2] Their collective spirit of fun is driven by all the employees and supported by a culture of open communication, trust and respect.

When I asked various Zappos employees (including the shuttle van driver who picked me up at my hotel) what drew them to Zappos, their answers all reflected the same theme:

> "They have an awesome culture."
>
> "They care about their employees and they have a wicked amount of fun."
>
> "I'm making less money than at my old job, but I'm three times as happy!"
>
> "It's the most fun and least amount of stress I've ever had working anywhere in my life!"

Companies such as Zappos demonstrate that Kevin Costner was on the right track when he built his field of dreams, with one small proviso: If you build it *right*, they really will come. In 2013, Zappos received 34,083 applications for 713 open positions. Many employees have relocated to work there. This shouldn't come as a surprise though: A 2012 Harris and Associates poll found that 75% of Canadians would move locations for the "right job." Similar numbers can be found in other countries around the world and given that the global labor force has never been more mobile than today, companies are no longer just competing for good talent with the shop around the corner.

The "right job" increasingly means working for a company that stands out from the herd with its culture. If you want to attract top talent and hire the best and brightest employees, you need to understand that the best and brightest employees can work for whoever they please. (It's one of the many awesome perks that go hand in hand with the whole "best and brightest" thing.)

Potential employees are now, more than ever, placing a premium on values other than money. In the heart of the twenty-first century, passion, meaning, creativity, work-life balance and *fun*, are as important—if not more so—as financial remuneration in choosing the right place to work. Companies such as Zappos needn't worry about tight labor markets: You don't need to go hunting once you've become the hunted.

Once you've branded yourself as a fabulous place to work, you can also afford to be picky. There are no shotgun weddings at Zappos. Like other inspiring organizations, Zappos understands that one of the keys to building a great workplace is to hire the right people: People who have a great attitude, are service-oriented and who have a healthy sense of humor.

As John Wolske says, "Yes, we have a fabulous culture, but Zappos still isn't for everyone. We have high standards and high expectations when it comes to our people. It's a different office environment. We foster an environment where employees spend a great deal of time together off hours as well. It really is a family—and that won't appeal to everyone."

This is one of the reasons new recruits are presented with a "Let's Make a Deal" scenario one week into their four-week-long orientation training, where every recruit is offered one month's salary to leave, no questions asked. It may sound like a gimmick, but Zappos does it with a very serious intent—to weed out those who aren't there for the right reasons. Even if lots of people took them up on their offer, it's a very modest investment. CEO Tony Hsieh has crunched his own numbers and believes that a bad hire can cost Zappos upward of one million dollars.

According to Mark Murphy, author of the book *Hiring for Attitude*, the focus that Zappos and other organizations have on attitude in their hiring is well-placed.[3] Of 20,000 new hires tracked by Murphy, 46% of them failed within eighteen months. But even more surprising than the failure rate was that when new employees failed, *89% of the time it was for attitudinal reasons* and only 11% of the time for a lack of skill. Shawn Achor, author of *The Happiness Advantage*, reports similar findings, suggesting that only 25% of job success is predicted by intelligence.[4] Meanwhile, a full 75% is based on three characteristics related to attitude: Optimism, a positive social network and a positive response to stress.

A study by the Consortium for Research on Emotional Intelligence also supports these findings. One study found that strong emotional competencies increased productivity by 85% to 127%. The L'Oreal company found that salespeople who were hired with a focus on emotional competency sold an average of $91,000 annually more than their peers who were hired via more traditional methods.[5]

## HIGH-FLYING FUN HELPS BUSINESSES SOAR

Other businesses are also finding recruitment success by blending a healthy dose of humor into their workplace mix. Calgary-based WestJet Airlines and Dallas-based Southwest Airlines are magnets for employees looking for a fun workplace culture.

Southwest Airlines has been a rebel in the airline business since its inception back in 1967. As the up-and-coming underdog fighting the behemoths, Southwest set out to build a different culture from the get-go: One that truly valued customers, cared passionately about their employees and had a whole lot of fun in the process. One of SWA's three overarching guiding principles for employees is to maintain a "Fun-Luving Attitude." ("Luving" because the stock symbol for Southwest Airlines is "LUV.")[6]

They even define what it means to embrace this kind of attitude at work:

- Have fun;
- Don't take yourself too seriously;
- Maintain perspective;
- Celebrate successes;

- Enjoy your work;
- Be a passionate team player.

It's those values that have sustained Southwest's success over the years and has helped them attract employees in outrageously high numbers. SWA spends a lot of money and effort in their recruiting, hiring and training practices, but it more than pays for itself: Southwest has one of the lowest employee turnover rates of any airline in the world.

When co-founder Herb Kelleher became chairman of SWA in 1978, he told their People Department to hire with a sense of humor in mind: "I want flying to be a helluva lot of fun. Life is too short and too hard and too serious not to be humorous about it!" Kelleher's call to action resulted in moving humor to the top of their hiring criteria; since then the company has staunchly adhered to the philosophy that you can train for all the rest, but you can't train for a fabulous attitude.

(Kelleher most famously demonstrated his belief in humor by settling a trademark dispute by arm wrestling another company's CEO. Several thousand people attended the highly publicized "Malice in Dallas" match at Dallas's Sportatorium, garnering national media attention and raising money for charities, to boot.)

Southwest gauges candidates' humor by asking such hiring questions as, "Tell us about a time you used humor to defuse a challenging situation?" or "Tell us how you've used humor recently in a work environment?"

On one famous occasion, a group of eight pilot applicants were teased about how seriously they were dressed in their dark suits and asked if they wouldn't be more comfortable changing into Southwest's standard issue Bermuda shorts. Six of the eight changed—the six that ended up getting hired. (For all the nervous flyers out there, rest assured that the airline's pilots still need to be able to fly the plane! But if they don't have a fantastic attitude to back up their technical competency, Southwest is not the place for them.)

Their branding starts with their recruitment efforts. Hiring ads in the past have featured images of Kelleher dressed as Elvis with a headline reading: "Work in a place where Elvis has been spotted. Send your resume Attention Elvis."

Despite the creative and offbeat hiring approach, Southwest still stresses that their employees work extremely hard. But the use of humor in their recruitment efforts and their branding as a fun place to work encourages a flood of applicants, many of whom resort to rather quirky applications being submitted over the years: Delivered on cereal boxes, filled in with a crayon, or even mounted on the top of a pizza box.

Similarly, it helps to have a sense of humor to become a "WestJetter" with WestJet Airlines. WestJet seeks out recruits with a good sense of humor because one of their core values is fun. But it works both ways: The reason WestJet is such an attractive employer is because they've followed Southwest's flight path and branded themselves as a fun airline, in stark contrast to the more staid, corporate image of Air Canada, their main competitor.

Even if you're only in the market for a few employees, a little humor can help make your business soar and improve the quality of your hires. That's what Barry Williams, the former manager of Barney's Motel in Brandon, Manitoba found after he upped the level of humor in his business.[7] Williams recognized that his two-star motel adjacent to the Trans-Canada Highway was never going to compete with the likes of Ritz-Carlton. So he decided to add some self-deprecating humor to his business and saw results immediately. One of the many areas where Williams made use of humor was in his help-wanted ads:

> *You love to clean... on weekends... for no wages. What... are you crazy? Why are you doing this for free when you could be making large coin at our place?*
>
> *Travel the world! Learn about exotic places! Well, okay, clean the rooms of people who travel the world, and learn about exotic places from them while you clean the rooms.*

Not only did ads such as these make Barney's Motel a hit with the locals who looked forward to reading his ads (even if they were already gainfully employed), Williams found that he started attracting people with a better attitude and healthier sense of humor.

## AN INSPIRING PRESCRIPTION FOR JOB DESCRIPTIONS

Job descriptions are rapidly becoming so *yesterday*. More and more organizations are eschewing formal job descriptions, opting instead for... well, nothing. Why? Because job descriptions too often box people in. They can become a subtle, or sometimes not-so-subtle, way of telling people what they *can't* do and help fuel the archaic, silo-creating, productivity-sapping, mind-numbingly annoying, "It's not in my job description" mentality so prevalent during the Jurassic period (*that's* the real reason dinosaurs died out).

If you must have job descriptions, ask yourself this: Do they energize people? Are they visionary, hopeful, daring, challenging, creative, unconventional, fun? Do they open doors or close doors? Do they connect people to a meaningful sense of purpose? Do they get people thinking about the possibilities of where their work could take them? Are they fun to read and conversational or dry as a Saharan rash? If you use your job descriptions for recruitment purposes, will they attract the right candidates with the right attitude for your workplace?

Here's the first part of a job description for a position with Woot, an online retail company that understands the importance of a compelling shout-out to potential employees:

> "You're so bright, people mistake you for the Greek god Apollo. You're so adept at multi-tasking, you're reading this while juggling. You're so self-motivated, your application is half-submitted and you haven't even gotten to the requirements yet! You love details, you crush deadlines, you organize like a Trapper Keeper and you switch gears like Steve McQueen at Le Mans. Discrete like Bond, professional like Jobs, and with the kind of humor that means you understand why a job description should be fun to read!"

Okay. I know what you're thinking: "OK, OK. I get that a bit of humor can work splendidly when you're managing a two-star motel, airline or amusement park, but surely humor could never be considered the weapon of choice for *more serious* career recruitments?"

## SOCIAL BRANDING: THE NEW RECRUITING GROUND

Cue the Hollywood-style cinematography, heart-pounding scenes of soldiers and an impossibly deep movie trailer voiceover:

> "We can't offer you an epic opening scene in which models pose like Marines. We can't offer you the opportunity to suddenly rise out of water holding some weird, futuristic weapon. We can't offer you a top secret hit-and-run mission in unknown territory. We can't offer you ridiculous dramatic music playing in the background, or even my cool American voice."

This award-winning video that blatantly pokes fun at over-the-top American military ads, is the recruitment video for the Swedish military. The video ends with the text: "But we *can* offer you our reality. An education that leads to a job where you can make a difference. For real. Welcome to *our* reality."

Speaking of reality, the new frontier for organizations seeking to attract great employees is, of course, the internet. Just as potential job candidates are using their LinkedIn, Twitter, Facebook and the Next Big Social Media Thingie accounts to promote their talents to organizations, employers are increasingly turning to the web to seek out good talent, screen candidates (*Dude, you actually posted that on Facebook?*) and, perhaps most importantly of all, to brand themselves as a fun place to work.

But before we get to the dancing Manila supermarket workers and lip-synching accountants, let's back up the whole branding bus for a moment and start with the basics.

As I've said already, you can't fake a great culture for very long before people catch on that it's all an act. If you want to brand your organization as people-centered, inspiring and fun, your branding needs to be consistent, pervasive and most importantly, backed up by actions.

So ask yourself these questions: When employees shopping for their next job drop by your website, are they treated to the usual, bland corporate double-speak? Are would-be hires (not to mention your customers, partners and vendors) suffering from the blahs when they read all the "blah, blah, blah" on your website? Do your vision and mission statements truly inspire and engage people, or do they read like the punch line in a Dilbert cartoon? (Of the hundreds of vision and mission statements I read each year, there are perhaps two or three that get my motor running. But shouldn't something as important as a vision statement get people's motors running?)

Incidentally, an inspiring and captivating vision statement that stands out from the herd isn't a trivial point. A 2013 Mercer survey found that 64% of employees believed a strong sense of purpose in their work was the most important motivational influence, beating out every other traditional employee perk with the exception of a good pension.[8]

If you want to attract top-notch talent, review your vision and mission statements, values, help-wanted ads and "about us" sections on your website to see how they might be coming across to potential employees. Are you using real, conversational language? Are you appealing to employees' hopes, dreams and desires? If cultural values are often trumping financial considerations for job-seekers, are you honestly spelling out how your culture rocks compared to your competitors?

Remember: Your culture is potentially your #1 competitive advantage—*but only if people are aware of it!*

That's where humor is lending a hand to so many businesses as they strive to stand out from the herd. Not only does humor help attract more attention, the use of self-deprecating humor is a brilliantly effective way to humanize your brand and help your organization come across as more real and more honest.

Hence the success of the Swedish military recruitment video: By poking fun at the American ads they're effectively saying: "We respect that you are intelligent enough to see through the hype of a traditional ad and we respect you enough to be honest with you about what you're really signing up for."

## WHO ARE YOU CALLING A DIRT BAG?

DIRTT Environmental Solutions, a construction company based in Calgary, Alberta, has built an inspiring and fun culture that has helped their business attract talent and laugh all the way to the bank (DIRRT, incidentally, is an acronym for Doing It Right This Time). The company has been recognized as one of the top-fifty best-managed companies in Canada and, yes, their employees are affectionately known as DIRTTbags. Here's how they describe themselves on their website:

> "Yep, we're DIRTTbags—you gotta problem with that? We are a passionate group of people spread out all over North America who would love nothing more than to see drywall sleepin' with da fishes. We strive to provide clients with the best solutions, experiences and environments possible. We help each other. We volunteer. We are often goofy. We all thrive on the idea that we are actually doing something to make the world a better place."

Cruise over to the career section of their website and you'll get more of a sense of what a career with DIRTT might be like:

> "Do you have what it takes to be a DIRTTbag? DIRTT Environmental Solutions is an unconventional company (this is a term we use in polite circles). We have no HR Department. Instead we run a Talent Agency where people—known affectionately as DIRTTbags—don't face lengthy policies, procedures or forms. What they do find is a highly motivated group of individuals who embrace the entrepreneurial spirit of DIRTT. Everyone is hands on, regardless of position. We celebrate our successes together. We have fun. We work hard. We respect each other. We achieve what others only dream about."

You can hear an actual human being's voice in their descriptions. They are playful and serious at the same time. They speak to their values and to the sense of purpose that so many people long for.

Touring their offices, one immediately gets a sense that DIRTT isn't faking it. Their offices are truly welcoming with funky meeting rooms, a cozy and inviting lounge area and inspiring quotes on the walls.

I sat down with two of the DIRTTbags, Jason Robinson and Janna Pantella, in their lounge, to discuss their culture. I'd like to be able to tell you their job titles, but they don't have any.

"We back up everything we say on our website," Robinson told me. "It really is all about culture here and we really do have some goofy fun. And yup, there are no job titles and no thick policy manuals. We let our actions do the talking."

"But," Pantella quickly added, "People also work extremely hard here. Which is why it's important to celebrate success and to keep building a fun and innovative culture."

Like most successful organizations, the spirit of fun starts at the top—you've got to love a company where the president has been pied in the face by the board of directors and the CEO has been pied by the employees. "Lounge Thursdays," where employees gather for a refreshing beverage in their office lounge, fun family events, charity team-building events, pumpkin-carving contests, a curse jar to raise money for charity (rumor has it they raise a lot of money) and paper airplane contests are regular fixtures that serve to build a sense of team spirit and tradition at DIRTT.

To make sure they bring aboard the right people, DIRTT managers spend as much time talking about their own culture during job interviews as they do assessing the candidates. They let people know that it's a "work hard, play hard" kind of environment where employees often debate ideas passionately and where, because it's the construction business, the humor can sometimes be a bit on the colorful side. (Okay, perhaps a lot on the colorful side.)

"Because we are so big on dressing up on Halloween here, I once conducted a job interview while dressed as an egg," Pantella confessed. "I think that gave the candidate a pretty good sense as to what our culture is like."

Of course, most organizations go to a great deal of effort to screen *out* the true dirt bags. So why not, as Red Door Interactive has done, brand yourself as an attractive place to work, send a powerful message about your core values and screen out less desirable candidates all at the same time?

Red Door Interactive, a marketing firm that's perennially listed as one of the best places to work in San Diego, offers prospective employees the promise of a "100% jerk-free" work environment. This slightly cheeky promise speaks volumes about their brand and culture and appeals to anyone who's ever had to put up with an annoying co-worker or obnoxious client.

The CEO, Reid Carr, stresses that the "100% jerk-free" promise is truly that.[9] Like any good company that backs up its values, it is treated as a commitment: They simply don't tolerate employees or clients who behave like jerks.

As Carr told me, "The funny and somewhat amazing thing is that some people self-screen themselves out of jobs during the job interview. So it not only helps make us distinct, it helps weed out the bad apples!"

## DOES YOUR JOB MAKE YOU WANT TO DANCE?

Okay, back to the dancing Manila supermarket workers. Why would SM City Supermarkets post a video on YouTube showing their employees line dancing in one of their supermarkets during the middle of a work day?

For the same reason the Swedish military is lobbing humor grenades at the Americans, why Cpl Jobs of Ireland posted their "Why We're a Great Place to Work" bloopers video, why the Adobe office in Germany posted a video of employees singing a parody of the "Boom De Yada" song, or why Hyatt has a video of employees from around the globe holding up fun signs expressing why they love working for the company.

From lip-synching custodians belting out the latest Lady Gaga number to gyrating accountants (there's a phrase you don't hear every day... and probably don't want to hear every day), businesses are desperately trying to outmaneuver their competitors and dance their way into the hearts and minds of potential employees.

Hence the explosion of "Life at _____" videos popping up on websites. What better way, after all, to give employees a sense of your culture *and* send the message that you can laugh at yourself by hamming it up for the cameras? Ericsson India, as just one of countless examples, has a "Life at Ericsson" video that showcases employees laughing, dancing and dressed in funny costumes.

The online matchmaking company Zoosk has a whole suite of videos that help brand itself as a fun, great place to work, including a hilarious recruitment video starring its own employees that promises to "put the casual back into business casual." (Any company that can make their engineers look like they have a fabulous sense of humor must be doing something right.)

A "Working at Google" video offers up a fast-paced look at life inside one of the coolest work environments on the planet, where prospective job candidates are invited to, "Do Something Cool that

Matters." The video offers a behind-the-scenes peek at the famous Googleplex headquarters in Mountain View, California, describing it as "one giant fun house." Employee testimonials interspersed with scenes of barbecues, restaurants serving up free food, fitness facilities, insanely funky meeting rooms, spa rooms, sleeping pods (and more) is sure to give a lot of cubicle-dwelling workers a serious case of office envy. And incidentally, the video has garnered close to two million views. That's a lot of envy and a lot of potential talent Googling the phrase, "How do I apply for a job at Google?"

## BUT SERIOUSLY, WHY DO PENGUINS WEAR SOMBREROS?

So imagine you are among the fortunate few lucky enough to make it to an interview with Google and they ask you the following question, "How many cows are in Canada?"

Interviews at Google might lob a question out of left field such as this to gauge your reaction and how you think through problems. There's a growing trend toward interviewers lobbing quirky questions out during job interviews.

For example, "A penguin walks into the room right now wearing a sombrero. What does he say and why is he here?" This question was posed during a job interview by Clark Construction for an office engineer position.

Or take this head-scratcher posed during a MasterCard interview: "Can you say 'Peter Piper Picked a Peck of Pickled Peppers' and cross sell a washing machine at the same time?"

Questions such as these are less direct than Southwest's humor questions, but the goal is often the same: To see how candidates cope with a curveball, assess their creative thinking skills and gauge their sense of humor. After all, there isn't one right answer to the penguin question (although wouldn't it be funny if there was?).

No credible interviewer is expecting a Seinfeld-worthy response. These companies aren't hiring stand-up comedians; they're trying to assess the candidate's attitude by considering the global definition of humor: Can the person respond to a funny question with a bit of a laugh and not take it overly seriously? Can the candidate laugh at themselves? Can they think outside... the sombrero?

The candidate who responds with a chuckle and replies with a bit of humor is likely going to make a far better impression than the dour fun-sucker who takes the question literally and points out that a penguin this far removed from Antarctica would likely never survive and someone really oughta call PETA and, by the way, dressing animals up in costumes is stupid and frankly, personally objectionable.

Speaking of animals in costumes, or conversely, humans who wear animal costumes, even the wonderful world of Disney reminds us that at the root of all this humor is a desire to build a great business. Lee Cockerell, the former Operations VP for Walt Disney World Resort, told me that the behind-the-scenes motto of Disney is, "The happiest place on earth... *or else.*"[10] Translation: Yes, Disney is all about the fun, but that doesn't mean they don't have extremely high expectations of their employees—expectations that are communicated to employees even *before* they apply for a job. People hoping to land a job with Disney must answer 132 questions online and watch a twenty-minute film before they are even interviewed! This helps ensure that Disney hires people with the right attitude who, in turn, begin their job understanding the high expectations demanded of them.

While we're on the subject of high expectations and fun, don't think for a moment that you need to choose one over the other when building a great business. It's not about fun or high expectations; it's about having fun while maintaining high expectations. There's a chicken-and-egg relationship here as well: If you have high expectations then it helps to have more fun and conversely, what's more fun than working in an organization that demands the very best?

## IT ALL LOOPS BACK TO BRANDING

Quick, what comes to mind when you think of IBM? For most, "Big Blue" likely conjures up such terms as, "conservative," "corporate," or "staid." But what about self-deprecating? Humble? Seriously funny? What if I told you that *Comedy Central* chose a series of online videos posted by IBM as one of their staff favorites in their comedy test pilot contest?

Taking a page from the sitcom *The Office,* IBM produced a series of self-deprecating, "mockumentary" videos and posted them online. "The Art of the Sales" video series was shot in-house, starring

IBM employees, in only a day and a half. The hilarious, deadpan videos immediately went viral. They've been viewed by hundreds of thousands of people, translated into several languages, used at sales conferences around the globe and have garnered IBM copious amounts of free publicity. The videos were a brilliant way to lighten up IBM's image and put a more human face on the company.

Similarly, Integris Credit Union, in central British Columbia, has created a series of online videos called "Banks, No Thanks!" that star their own employees in some very offbeat, funny videos. In one video, Employee Engagement & Communications Manager Alex Castley emerges from a lake dressed in a business shirt and tie, dramatically shaking his wet head in slow motion before launching into some of the benefits of their credit union, only to be distracted by a giant squirrel. Outrageously funny and definitely most unexpected from a financial institution.

Pop quiz time. Who were the IBM and Integris Credit Union videos produced for?

A. Existing employees in need of a morale boost;
B. Potential hiring candidates considering their career options;
C. Existing clients, partners and vendors;
D. Future clients and customers;
E. All of the above.

If you answered *All of the above*, give yourself the rest of the day off! (I'm sure it's okay with your boss and if it's not, have her call me.)

It's difficult to know where the line is when it comes to branding efforts: Are companies doing it to attract and keep great employees or loyal customers? In reality, there really isn't a line. *The Art of the Sales* video series conveys a branding message to IBM employees *and* their customers. Line dancing nurses send a message to potential employees *and* patients. The Southwest Airlines' flight attendant who famously raps the safety message (another viral YouTube sensation) helps forge an image that appeals to both customers *and* recruits.

As Integris's Alex Castley told me, "The original intent of the funny videos was to help us reach a younger demographic as an attractive place to work, but we see now that they are also great marketing and branding videos. In positioning them as marketing videos, we feel potential employees will be naturally attracted to the videos—and us—as well."

In fact, shouldn't one of your goals be to build the kind of business where your customers, suppliers or partners—like the delivery guy at Zappos—want to become employees? Where your employees actually want to do business with you and serve as passionate goodwill ambassadors on behalf of your company? To build a great workplace *and* attract and retain loyal customers, organizations need to attract and hire employees with the right attitude. As we've seen, to attract top talent with the right attitude, it helps to brand yourself as a great place to work.

Of course, attracting great employees is merely step one on the journey toward outrageously inspiring success.

The real work—and the real fun—is just beginning.

### Key Messages and Ideas

1. Culture drives success. Your culture is potentially your #1 competitive advantage.
2. Great cultures don't happen by accident. To build an inspiring culture you need to be *intentional.*
3. Humor is a key ingredient in an inspiring culture. The use of humor in the workplace *drives* success and *reflects* success at work.
4. Humor can help brand any organization as a great place to work to help it stand out from the herd and attract great employees.
5. To build an inspiring culture and a successful business, hire for attitude and for people who have a healthy sense of humor.
6. Rewrite your job descriptions for all your employees to make them as meaningful, as engaging and as fun as possible.
7. Along the lines of Zappos' "Director of First Impressions," "Lead Culture Guide," or the "DIRTTbags" at DIRTT Environmental Solutions, create fun job titles, titles that reflect the true nature

of the work. If you feel your environment is too conservative to allow such titles, at least assign alternative job titles (they can always go on the back of everyone's business cards).

8. Create a fun recruitment video that will help brand your business and get your business noticed by the world. (If the Swedish military can do it, anyone can do it.)
9. Create a fun "Life at ________" video starring your own employees that will give potential candidates a sense of your workplace culture.

# 3

# Building a Tribal Culture That's a Barrel of Laughs

"Work and play are words used to describe the same thing under differing conditions."

– Mark Twain

Imagine what a thrill it must be to walk the red carpet, smile for the cameras and wave at the adoring fans waiting just for *you*. Only a few people get to experience such a high: Brad and Angelina, Madonna, Sting and, of course, Bob... the new computer engineer at technology giant Intel.

Every quarter, as part of their Red Carpet Experience, new Intel employees walk the red carpet, lined with Intel photographers and videographers, before heading on to a stage to receive their welcome packages and a rousing greeting from fellow employees. The new hires are made to feel like a million bucks, which only makes sense given the millions of bucks companies spend annually to replace unhappy employees who vote themselves off their respective islands.

Intel understands that if you want to attract and *keep* great employees, building a committed relationship starts on day one (especially when you consider a rather frightening survey that found some new hires start looking for a new job *within three days* of starting any job).

Number crunchers suggest that every time a person walks out the front door for greener pastures it costs at least twice their salary to replace them. Add to that whopping cost associated with the loss of experience and knowledge, the added stress on existing employees, plus the negative press you'll be stung with if that employee leaves with a bad taste in his or her mouth and it's shocking that companies don't focus more efforts on building a thriving culture that places a premium on employee happiness and well-being.

## YOU HAVE TO HAND IT TO THIS BOOK

"Dedicated to the families of all Valve employees. Thanks for making us such an incredible place." So reads the inspiring dedication in the gaming company Valve's *Handbook for New Employees*, subtitled: "A fearless adventure in knowing what to do when no one's there telling you what to do."

Someone who reads that on day one of their new job likely won't suffer from "hire's remorse," which is similar to buyer's remorse but with much deeper and longer-lasting consequences for both employer and employee. Valve's new employee handbook (wisely posted on their website for the world to see) includes cartoons, fun diagrams and a healthy dose of humor. It's conversational and unconventional. The handbook gives new employees a very real understanding of Valve's culture. It's unabashedly honest, even telling employees what the company *doesn't* do very well!

The handbook includes a glossary of company lingo, which also offers a sense of its playful culture:

> *Company Vacation*: Every year, the company gathers all the employees and our families, flies us somewhere tropical and gives us a free week-long vacation. Popular pastimes include beard contests, snorkeling, ice cream socials and jet skiing, or just sitting on the beach chatting with the locals about how many googly-eyed seashells you should buy from them.
>
> *Manager*: The kind of people we don't have any of. So if you see one, tell somebody, because it's probably the ghost of whoever was in this building before us. Whatever you do, don't let him give you a presentation on paradigms in spectral proactivity.

Valve's new employee handbook is intended to promote *and* reflect the company culture it wants to sustain.

With a similar goal in mind, the Peabody Hotel in Orlando, Florida asks their new employees to sign a "Grumpy Pledge" wherein they vow not to come into work grumpy. It may sound a tad cheesy, but it's a light-hearted way of conveying expectations and reminding new hires of an important message: "Remember during the job interview, when you told us you had an awesomely positive attitude? Well, we'd like you to keep that promise. So sign here. Initial here, here and here. And one more signature next to the smiley face."

Once again there's more to this than meets the twinkling eye. A study by Dr. James Fowler of the University of California found that bad moods are highly contagious.[1] Each unhappy interpersonal connection a person makes decreases the chances of that person being happy by 7%, so it's well worth the effort to try and de-grump-ify your workplace starting on day one.

## INITIATING THE UNINITIATED

At DIRTT, new employees are initiated into the fold with what's become a bit of a tradition. Admittedly, "initiation" is a bit of a loaded term, but if done properly and with a good-hearted spirit, friendly workplace initiations can become time-honored traditions that make new employees feel like they are part of the team. In fact, a study reported in the *International Journal of Humor Research* found that workplace kidding and teasing play an important role in team bonding: We tend to kid people we are closest to, so teasing someone conveys the message, "You're one of us now."

The key to success is to do something that won't embarrass or humiliate the employee, result in a lawsuit or injury, or result in the employee having a severe case of hire's remorse to the point that they run out your front door screaming in abject terror. (You think I jest, but a young mechanic in Australia was left with burns on his body after a workplace initiation prank involving solvents went horrifically awry!)

DIRTT's initiation may, in fact, inflict a temporary state of hire's remorse, but it fits their playful culture to a tee. New employees are told they have to do a presentation in front of all the employees at their next weekly Thursday lounge afternoon and that past presentations have ranged from sock puppet shows to skits. The never-overly-thrilled new employee is left to stew for several hours until moments before their big show is scheduled to hit the stage, when they are finally informed that there is no tradition of new employee presentations. Cue the relief. The key to making this practical joke work? The new employee gets to mete out their revenge by being the person to sucker in the *next* new employee.

If you fear practical joke-style initiations might steer you into uncharted waters, here's just a sample of a few fun ways companies welcome employees into the fold with some good humor:

- Cxtec has new employees serve coffee and donuts to all the employees on the first Friday of every month as a way of encouraging them to meet everyone in a fun way.
- Several companies have new employees wear a colored name tag for the first month, so other employees can be on the lookout for them and welcome them properly.
- Try an employee scavenger hunt, wherein new hires have one month to match various offbeat personal attributes, talents and trivia tidbits to all the employees.
- Create a fun Welcome Survival Kit that includes some office toys, funny props and humorous reading material that will help the employee cope with the demands of the new job.
- A welcome package sent home to the families of new employees makes a fabulous statement—remember they are now an important part of your support team.
- One company hires a cartoonist to draw a caricature of new employees, which then gets framed and posted outside their office or cubicle (Not to worry, if the employee doesn't like the drawing they are allowed a do-over!)

Red carpet ceremonies, company handbooks, funny pledges, initiations and employee scavenger hunts can all help create a fabulous first impression for new employees. But let's face it, anyone can make a good first impression. Aren't we, after all, at our shiniest best on a first date?

The real test begins when the honeymoon is over.

## A BERYL OF LAUGHS

Beryl Companies, a health care call center in Bedford, Texas, knows all too well the high cost associated with employee turnover. Call centers are notorious for poor working conditions and one of the highest employee turnover rates of any industry, which is one of the reasons Beryl's HR Manager, Lara Morrow, proudly holds the alternative job title of "The Queen of Fun and Laughter."[2]

As with Zappos and Southwest Airlines, Beryl eschews the shotgun-wedding approach to hiring; instead they strive to ensure there's a long-term love connection between candidate and company. As with Zappos, they routinely "back check" hiring candidates to assess how they interacted with employees on the way to the job interview.

"It's like Ft. Knox to get a job with us," Queen Morrow told me. "You might even say it's a pain in the butt. But you know what's a bigger pain in the butt? Getting rid of someone who isn't a fit for our culture! We try to nurture a long-term relationship from day one."

This is why they're especially cautious when hiring anyone for a leadership position, going so far as to take potential candidates out to lunch to observe how they interact with the service staff. As Morrow said, "How people treat kids, dogs and service staff is a pretty good indicator of their true character."

So despite the fact that Beryl is known for its fun, family-friendly culture, it's not easy to get a job with them. But once you're on the inside, they'll take care of you like you're a treasured member of their family. Beryl leaders focus relentlessly on treating employees right, on showing them that they care about their well-being and on having fun.

A workplace committee, the Better Beryl Bureau, helps drive events and support the work of employees who want to get involved in creating that spirit of fun. Regular employee barbeques are par for the course (they are in Texas, after all) but the spirit is also embraced through wacky hat days, special events that include family members (more than 500 of their employees' children celebrate Halloween at their office each year), crazy videos starring Beryl executives, an annual gong show talent night and a "Dancing with the Executives" event.

CEO Paul Spiegelman stresses two fundamental reasons to emphasize the injection of a good dose of levity into the workplace: It's good for business and it's the right thing to do. "Our fun and caring culture is the key to growing our business," said Spiegelman. "It's our #1 competitive advantage and the key to attracting and keeping the right employees."

According to the book *Happiness at Work* by Jessica Pryce-Jones, Beryl's strategy of focusing on employee happiness and well-being really does pay off: Happy workers use 66% less sick leave, are 50% more motivated and 50% more productive.[3] James Heskett, a professor at Harvard University Graduate School of Business Administration, also found that companies that distinguish themselves in how they hire, train and ultimately treat their employees experience growth rates 30 – 300% greater than their competitors and that an effective culture can account for up to half of the differential in performance between organizations in the same business.[4]

Despite the fact that there was an obvious business case to be made, it was clear to me that Spiegelman's passion for his employees came from a deeply personal place. When I asked him what the light-bulb moment was that made him decide to run his business in such an unorthodox manner, he chuckled. "Everyone asks that question. But the truth is there was no light-bulb moment. We've been like this since day one because I didn't know any different—I actually thought this was how all businesses operated until I started hearing from employees that this is *not* the normal reality out there in the wide world of work!"

Tied to his commitment to employees is Spiegelman's passion for the arts, which he shares with employees through Beryl's monthly outings to various local events and attractions—all on Beryl's dime and open to anyone who wants to take advantage of it. The popular Saturday outings include trips to art museums, wine tastings and concerts.

Their passionate and relentless focus on building a vibrant and fun culture has reduced Beryl's turnover rate to less than 13% in an industry where the average turnover rate approaches 80% in some markets. It has also helped drive phenomenal business growth: Beryl nets *five times* the profit of their closest competitors.

You might be thinking that it's easy to have an inspiring culture when you've started out that way, but just how easy is it to turn an entire ship around that didn't have the storied launch of a Zappos, Southwest Airlines, or Beryl?

## TURNING YOUR WORKPLACE SHIP AROUND

The USS Benfold is a guided-missile destroyer (whew, sounds like a barrel of laughs already) that was commanded by Captain D. Michael Abrashoff for twenty months beginning in 1997. As he details in his book, *It's Your Ship: Management Techniques from the Best Damn Ship in the Navy,* Abrashoff was able to increase the crew retention rate from a dismal 28% to an outstanding 100% by nurturing a more positive culture, which included—even in the "rules-and-discipline-are-everything" military—having more fun aboard the ship.[5] They brought aboard a karaoke machine. They held theme days and kite-flying contests. They looked for ways to make mundane duties more engaging. The crew worked hard, but they had fun along the way.

One story Abrashoff recounted to me illustrates the nature of their team-building humor:

> "We had a wonderful Command Master Chief (CMC) by the name of Bob Scheeler. He's the senior enlisted guy and he represents the crew. He would be the shop steward if we had unions on the ship. I had endless amounts of fun at his expense. He was a good egg about it but by investing so much attention on him, it showed the crew that he had a seat at the table and that the crew knew I would always take their viewpoint into account because of my wonderful relationship with him... their representative. His stature, in their eyes, grew and grew.
>
> We had a closed-circuit television system on the ship that I commandeered to send messages to the crew. I put the news on it, sports scores, you name it—it was must-see TV as soon as you woke up in the morning. This was back in the days of personal ads as a medium of meeting people and one morning, I colluded with our TV operator to post a personal ad that would come up while the crew was eating breakfast and watching the news.
>
> It was something like "MWCMC" (Married White Command Master Chief) ISO (in search of) lonely sailors looking to advance their careers. Meet me on the fantail after sunset for a moonlight stroll....

> It was a riot. The crew howled. The Chief Petty Officers were outraged that I would so publicly make fun of their leader. In retaliation, they kidnapped my docksider shoes from my cabin while I was working out one day... and every day for a week they submitted ransom notes in the form of cutout letters from magazines. Turns out, they had taped my purloined and beloved docksiders underneath my seat at the dinner table where they were for an entire week while I held an inquisition for them."

Having more fun certainly wasn't the only key to their success. Abrashoff writes passionately about the need for leaders to see the ship from the eyes of the crew and on the importance of listening, celebrating a sense of purpose and communicating, communicating and communicating. But adding fun to the mix was also a key ingredient that helped them build the kind of cohesive, team-oriented culture that drove impressive results. As he said, "Through laughter, you can show people you are human and that goes a long way these days in the workplace. People just want to know that you are human." The fact that Commander Abrashoff was able to turn his ship around bodes well for any workplace culture in need of a reboot. And sometimes, that turnaround can happen surprisingly fast.

## ACT NOW!

AFA JCDecaux is the largest outdoor advertising company in the world, with offices in more than fifty-nine countries. A huge success by many measures, the company had nevertheless lost its mojo a few years ago.

When I met with CEO Kim Axelson in his Copenhagen, Denmark boardroom, the first thing I noticed was the welcoming plate of fresh food and delicious-looking Danishes (Hey, I was hungry. And who wouldn't want to eat a Danish Danish?). The second thing I noticed was the bright yellow sign on the meeting room wall adorned with the text: "Blah, blah, blah... ACT NOW!"

Axelson vibrated with energy as he shared the company's success story and explained how they hit the reset button and revitalized their workplace culture in a mere four months: "That sign says it all! If you just get off your duff and commit to action great things can happen!"

So how did they shake things up?

They started by revamping their company values from the ground up—employees created the values themselves, ensuring immediate buy-in from everyone. They came up with four values:

1. Teamwork;
2. Create positivity;
3. Show a fighting spirit;
4. Create humor.

To turn those words into action, the company honed in on one value each week, asking every employee to embrace and champion the "value of the week" as passionately as possible, cycling through the four and then repeating the process for six months. By encouraging an intensive, all-hands-on-deck approach that even the USS Benfold would be proud of, they hoped the values would become better understood and completely ingrained into everyone's behaviors.

The results spoke for themselves: absenteeism rates dropped by 30%, while employee retention rates improved by 25%. Axelson said that within only four months—before they had even finished their six-month process—things were different. *Substantially* different.

"We became a new company!" Axelson said, grinning ear to ear. "This stuff is simple. You just need to do it and give people the freedom to act with passion and to act immediately when they have a great idea!"

A central part of the cultural shift involved a dedicated effort to infuse the workplace with more humor. Signs and posters with slogans reading, "We Want *You* to Have Fun" and life-sized posters of happy businesspeople reminded everyone to lighten up. A squadron of employees went so far as to visit employees' homes one Sunday, leaving signs and stickers reminding them to find the humor in their lives. Back in the office, celebratory walls were created featuring photos of employees when they were born, during their wedding and doing fun things in their spare time. Computers were rigged to start up with a humorous message. Random, spontaneous fun breaks were injected into the workplace that included Salsa dancing lessons and a contest to eat the most dessert with employees' hands tied behind their backs. Team competitions, family celebrations and raving company testimonials in the internal newsletter all helped infuse a spirit of playfulness in the company.

As a simple way to gauge the mood in their main office and to remind people they had the power to choose their attitude, Plexiglas boxes were installed throughout the office. As employees went about their work day, they would drop in either a green rubber ball if they were feeling great about things, or a red ball if things weren't so good. A quick scan of the boxes gave managers an instant office mood barometer. If an employee sees a colleague place a few red balls in a container, others rally around to see if they can do anything to help.

As you'll see in Chapter Nine, the fun spilled over into how they interacted with their customers as well, resulting in increased business and a waiting list of people wanting a job with AFA JCDecaux. All because they turned their blah, blah, blah into inspired action.

## BUILDING A TRIBAL CULTURE WITH HUMOR

Sometimes a little monkey business at work is exactly what the culture doctor ordered. Particularly in the case of Winnipeg, Manitoba's Argus Industries. Starting every December 1, Argus has a ritual wherein an employee dressed in a gorilla costume hides in various places throughout the front offices and the manufacturing areas, waiting to pounce and frighten the bejeezus out of slightly suspecting employees. I say "slightly suspecting" because the employees know it's going to happen sometime in early December, they just don't know where or when. CEO and President Mike Easton told me with a rather mischievous grin on his face, "Starting on December 1, employees come into work with a certain amount of fear and trepidation." (Sounds similar to a job I had many years ago, only it was year-round and didn't involve any fun. But I digress.)

Merely scaring employees isn't the punch line, however. The real fun happens at the Argus annual Christmas bash where employees are treated to a video montage of all the frightened reactions, girlish screams (primarily from the men) and hysterical laughter surreptitiously caught on tape.

It's one of many Argus traditions that dovetails nicely into their overarching guiding philosophy: "Work is hard enough as it is without making it any harder!"

Argus CEO Mike Easton believes that the key to a great business lies in building what he calls a "tribal culture." They define a tribal culture as one where everyone feels cared for; valued and respected; where everyone has a voice. Part of forming a tribal culture, Easton suggests, is to make sure the tribe is having fun. Most importantly, it's an inclusive culture, where everyone feels they are part of a single team and the only silos to be seen are on Manitoba's prairie landscape.

Building a single tribe in an organization composed of many departments (often in different locations) is a challenge at the best of times. "We need to bust down our silos" is a common rallying cry from executives around the world and for good reason: Silos in the workplace contribute to poor communication, increased stress, reduced innovation and teams working at cross purposes to each other. Silos cost companies untold millions of dollars due to inefficiencies, duplicate processes and lost productivity.

As in the case of Argus Industries, it takes a concerted and multipronged effort to destroy silo walls. Committing to a powerful central vision, communicating your ass off (pardon my language, but really, that's what it takes), flattening your hierarchy, changing the physical layout of your office and minimizing bureaucratic processes all help reduce silos.

But adding a bit of monkey business clearly isn't a bad idea either.

One of the many tangible benefits of creating fun rituals at Argus has been to break down the traditional divide that existed between the white collar front-office employees and the blue collar back-office ones in their manufacturing plant. So mac n' cheese cook-offs, fun family events, lurking gorillas and theme days such as "monochromatic day" (where everyone dresses in only black and white) all help unify employees at Argus. Particularly effective at joining the front- and back-office employees has been their tradition of "X Game" competitions, where teams compete in fun work-related events that teach people the challenges of each other's jobs, resulting in new-found respect for the work everyone does.

The belief at Argus is that a team that laughs together works better together. When a group of workers share a laugh, walls evaporate: managers vs. employees, blue collar vs. white collar and us vs. them rivalries dissolve when people laugh together in a unifying experience.

Indeed, there's more to laughing as a group than meets the eye. According to Robert R. Provine, author of *Laughter: A Scientific Investigation,* "Laughter is the quintessential human social signal. Laughter is about relationships."[6]

Provine's research found that people laugh *thirty times more* when they are around other people than when they are alone. Numerous studies confirm that laughter is highly contagious, hence the whole point of canned laughter egging us on in TV sitcoms. Since it was first used to accompany *The Hank McCune Sho*w on September 9, 1950, the laugh track has, until very recently, been a staple of most sitcoms... despite the fact that a *Time* magazine article included the laugh track on their list of "The 100 Worst Ideas of the Century."

As much as laughter is a byproduct of social connectedness, it also contributes to social cohesion. Laughter, Provine found, plays a significant role in social bonding, solidifying friendships and pulling people into the fold. This is likely why laughter isn't as dependent on humor as you might have imagined. In fact, the vast majority of laughter happens without any humorous stimuli. People routinely inject laughter into their conversations and with good reason: Laughter, although largely involuntary, is thought to convey messages such as, "We're on the same team," "I mean you no harm," and (at least in my house) "Really, *that's* the shirt you're wearing tonight?"

Workplace studies reinforce the importance of shared humor and laughter. A year-long study of hotel kitchen workers demonstrated that even critical humor helped solidify groups by highlighting their shared beliefs.[7] A study of Sardinian fish market workers found that humor brought the workers closer together by reminding them of their commonalities.[8]

Even without the social cohesive benefits of laughter, fun traditions and rituals at work are critically important morale boosters. They help create a "want to" kind of workplace instead of a "have to" kind of workplace. Traditions give employees something to look forward to and something to reminisce about, two keys to boosting overall levels of happiness, experts say. Merely *anticipating* something positive boosts the level of dopamine in our brains, sometimes triggering more of a chemical reward than when we experience the event itself! As well, traditions and rituals create a sense of shared experiences and shared history which is so critical in building a strong culture.

Michael I. Norton, an associate professor at Harvard Business School and co-author of several studies on the importance of rituals, has found that those performed as a group make employees feel closer and more connected, resulting in a healthy boost to team performance.[9] A University of Michigan study found that people who tap into their sense of humor more frequently become more inclusive, thinking in terms of "us" versus "them."[10]

Rituals help employees succeed at an individual level as well: Employees who participate in a ritual before a difficult task are less anxious, get more involved and tend to perform better than people who don't have one.[11] So whether it's growing your beard for your team's playoff run, banging a giant gong every time a major sale is landed, or scaring co-workers in a gorilla suit, rituals and traditions are important ways to build a tribal culture.

Just how much of an impact can a tribal culture have on employees' well-being and a company's bottom line? Mike Easton relayed a story of how a senior manager at Argus had been headhunted by a competitor, with an offer of a substantially higher salary that Argus simply wasn't in a position to match. But in the end, it didn't matter. After talking it over with his spouse, the manager chose to stay at Argus. Why? Because, as the spouse pointed out, the employee had never been happier than when working at Argus.

There's no shortage of opportunities for traditions and rituals in the workplace. Even the stodgy New York Stock Exchange honors a fun spirit of tradition with their ritualized daily opening and closing of the trading day, dating back to the late 1800s when it was first done by a gavel, then a gong (far more fun in my humble opinion) and, since 1903, the bell still in use today. By featuring celebrities and prominent corporate executives at the bell ringing, the opening of trading is turned into a mini-event each and every day.

Rituals can take place daily, weekly, monthly, or yearly. You can create traditions to kick off the day, the week, the start of a quarter or the beginning of a new year. You can celebrate the end of the day, week, month, or year. You can create a tradition tied to each day of the week, rituals to kick off your meetings, or to end your meetings. You can create a tradition linked to launching a new product or program or even mourning the death of a program or obsolete product. And, as we'll explore in the next chapter, to create an inspiring culture you absolutely *must* create traditions tied to celebrating success, achieving key milestones and recognizing employees.

Here are six opportunities to create fun traditions and rituals in your workplace:

**1. Celebrating the Standard Holidays**—I'm speaking here of the usual suspects: Halloween, Independence Day, Canada Day, Thanksgiving and Christmas, with one important caveat: As workplaces become increasingly culturally diverse, it's important to recognize cultural differences when you celebrate some of these holidays. Even Halloween can be controversial.

A 2013 Glassdoor Talent Solutions survey found that 59% of employees feel doing something fun at the office for Halloween is good for morale.[12] But here's the tricky part: Some people love Halloween; some people *really* hate it. Although many employees are fine with decorating the office or bringing treats into work, according to the Glassdoor survey only 6% of employees enjoy bobbing for apples and only 11% would enjoy a costume parade around the office. Halloween is a great reminder of a universal principle when it comes to fun in the workplace: Ask for input on what everyone wants to do and then give everyone an equal *opportunity* to participate *without forcing them to participate*. After all, forcing people to have fun is akin to saying, "The beatings will stop once morale has improved."

So using Halloween as an example, why not use holidays as a time to do some charity work for children or, as Beryl has done so successfully, create a celebration for employees' families?

But holidays—even those with religious underpinnings—needn't create tension in a diverse workplace. There's a difference between recognizing that we have different beliefs and being frightened of those differences to the point that nobody moves for fear of offending someone. Instead, why not celebrate the differences? Use holidays as a golden opportunity to learn more about each other's heritage and traditions.

**2. Celebrate Non-standard Holidays and Theme Days—** For a listing of offbeat theme days, visit www.HumoratWork.com and type "wacky theme days" into the search box to find a list, sorted by month. Some of my favorites include what I'd call the more "traditional non-traditional days," such as Ground Hog Day and April Fool's Day and the "REALLY not-very-traditional days" such as: Show and Tell Day at Work; Answer Your Cat's Question Day; Do a Grouch a Favor Day; Make Up Your Own Holiday Day; International Moment of Laughter Day; Nerd Pride Day; Salute to Silliness Day; Take Your Dog to Work Day; Gruntled Workers Day; Sneak Zucchini onto Your Neighbor's Porch Day; Hug Your Boss Day; Talk Like a Pirate Day; Bring Your Teddy Bear to Work Day; Absurdity Day; High-Five Day; and Cat Herder's Day. Even if you do nothing more than write whatever wacky theme day it happens to be on a whiteboard at the entrance to your office, or include a mention on your voice mail message, it's a simple way to inject a bit of levity into everyone's day.

**3. Invent Your Own Theme Days—**I've had clients who've done everything from official "High-Five Day" once a month (fairly self-explanatory and very inexpensive) to "Fish Bowl Fridays" (where every person's name goes into a fishbowl and whichever name gets drawn gets to escape the corporate fishbowl an hour early). A bank does a theme day once a year wherein the employees get to decide what the supervisor will wear to work that day. Another bank holds "Laugh-in Luncheons" wherein employees watch reruns of classic sitcoms during lunch break every Friday. My favorite theme day has to be "Third-Person Thursdays," wherein everyone in the office must talk about themselves all day Thursday in the third person. (Mike loves this idea! Mike thinks this couldn't help but make people walk around with a smile on their faces all day!)

**4. Do Work for Charity—**Getting involved in a charity event is one of the best ways of building bonds in the workplace while instilling a sense of purpose and meaning in people's work. Every community has dozens of fun charity events that offer opportunities for team-building events, friendly competition and a chance to take a break from the office—and all for a worthy cause to boot. I've seen offices where even the women get on board the mustache-growing spirit of Movember to help raise awareness for prostate cancer by wearing fake mustaches for the month of November. Events like these help cement relationships, build team spirit and create countless moments of laughter and good humor.

**5. Hold Fun Contests**—From "Match the Employee to the Foot/Baby/High School Grad/Pet" photo contests to your own customized "Office Olympics," there's no shortage of fun contests that will help build team spirit. Indicative perhaps of a growing trend, Dartmouth professor Frank Zarnowski coined the phrase "work-sports" in reference to the growing number of work-skills competitions, including oyster-shucking contests, gift wrapping, lumberjack events and even grave-digging competitions!

You can devise fun contests that also help you achieve certain goals: Contests to create a new slogan for a new product or service, or one to come up with the best workplace theme song. Nugget Market, for example, holds a "Bag Off" contest to find the quickest bagger and a "Spirit Competition" to see which store can demonstrate the best company spirit. Microsoft has a "My Story" contest where employees are encouraged to submit a video of themselves explaining why Microsoft is a fun place to work. Including the families of employees in some of the contests is a great way to build your culture and engage the support team as well.

**6. Create a Rotating Corporate Jester Position**—Calgary-based Rogers Insurance has a Director of Humor position that employees must apply for by submitting a humor plan of attack. It's a rotating, four-month term position that comes with a small budget and a financial bonus at its end. The Director of Humor has to accomplish his or her fun duties in addition to their regular work and they must commit to a minimum number of events and activities. It's a simple way to keep the spirit of fun and humor alive and to remind everyone that they value humor in their culture.

Of course, some traditions don't fit neatly into a category, so here's a list of ten offbeat rituals to get your creative juices flowing:

> **10. Stealth Disco**—This is where an employee is interviewed on video by another colleague while a co-worker secretly disco dances behind them. It's like a photo bomb only with video. And disco.

**9. Play of the Day**—A product design team at Microsoft has a tradition wherein someone gets to choose the song of the day that gets blasted through the office at exactly 3 pm every day. Employees dance, sing along or, as necessary, berate the person for choosing a Celine Dion number.

**8. First One to Say "Good Morning!"**—This is inspired by a friend of mine, a former manager who got competitive with another manager about who was the first to greet the other one in the morning. This led to the two of them keeping score, which in turn led to them hiding in the parking lot, under desk tables, or in a closet first thing in the morning in order to be able to pounce out and notch another victory. Their game lasted eight years until the one manager got the other's wife to wake up in bed, loom right over his face and greet him with, "Larry says good morning." Game, set, match.

**7. Dancing with the Executives**—I've already mentioned this one, but it bears repeating here because it's so wacky. Beryl holds this annual event wherein they spoof Dancing with the Stars. Only instead of stars, it's, you know, your boss!

**6. Crazy Hour**—A good one to try at 3 pm every day to help energize folks suffering from a severe case of the afternoon blahs. Unlike happy hour, this just lasts five minutes. Employees are encouraged to do anything that gets them up off their duffs and acting goofy to generate some laughs. Human Dynamics, for example, has a tradition where everyone spins around in their chair at 3 pm for thirty seconds to get everyone laughing.

**5. Stupid Human Tricks**—A good one for every workplace to try once or twice a year and a great way to get to know where the ear wigglers, dolphin imitators, jugglers and closet mimes are hanging out in your office.

**4. Amateur Night**—Similar to Stupid Human Tricks, only this gives budding comedians a chance to shine. If you want to encourage more humor in your workplace and create some team-building events, what's better than hearing original comedy material from your colleagues? The Funniest Fed competition, an annual event in Washington, D.C. has turned this into a very popular fund-raising event. (As we'll see in Chapter Five, there's perhaps more to doing stand-up than meets the ear.)

**3. How You Doin'?**—This simple morning ritual works as follows: Everyone who works together on a team goes around the room first thing in the morning and yells out how they're doing on a scale of one to ten. This serves three purposes: Like the red or green rubber ball measure employed by AFA JCDecaux, it offers a quick assessment of the team temperature; it reminds people they have the power to choose their attitude each day and hit the reset button if need be; and it identifies anyone under a 5.0, who might need some extra team support.

**2. Monday Morning Kick-Off Messages**—Leave an inspiring or funny greeting on everyone's voice mail to greet them every Monday morning. It's a simple way to help people look forward to Monday mornings in some small way.

**1. Monthly Laugh Offs**—Admittedly, this one may be too "out there" for most people, but if part of the idea of creating traditions is to get teams laughing together more, try what some organizations are doing around the world and hold a laugh contest a few times a year where employees vie for the funniest, loudest, longest, most maniacal and most contagious laugh.

## GETTING TO KNOW YOU... GETTING TO KNOW ALL ABOUT YOU

To build a thriving team environment it obviously helps if people on the team like each other. Numerous studies on employee happiness and well-being have found that a key factor is whether or not they have close friends in their workplace. A Randstad survey, for example, found that 67% of workers reported having friends at work makes their job more fun and enjoyable, while 55% feel that these relationships make their job more worthwhile and satisfying.[13] A survey by Jobsite of 1,000 U.K. workers found that having friends at work was the most important factor in job happiness for 70% of the respondents.[14]

Research from Gallup also supports this, suggesting that there's only a one in twelve chance of an employee being fully engaged in work if they have no close friends at work.[15] On the other hand, having at least three friends at work increases engagement and life satisfaction by a whopping 96%. Yet, Gallup also found that fewer than 20% of organizations recognize the value of friendships at work.

Surveys also reveal that most employees feel a far greater loyalty to their own team than to the organization at large. This isn't something to be feared; it simply reflects the fact that we are all most loyal to the people closest to us. It should, in fact, be encouraged. Strong team loyalty can help smooth over larger organizational bumps in the road: If employees feel a strong enough attachment and loyalty to their team, they're more likely to remain positive and stay with a company when it hits a rough patch.

Although it undoubtedly helps boost productivity and team cohesiveness when employees like each other, we all know it's not going to happen all the time. What *is* important when it comes to building a cohesive team is nurturing a culture that fosters mutual trust and respect. One of the key ways to do that is by ensuring that employees get to know the real humans lurking behind job titles and functions, which is where humor can help: As I've said, we're never more real than when we laugh.

Numerous studies demonstrate that people with shared interests or personality traits are slightly more inclined to favor each other. A bond can be formed over the smallest of similarities: a love of pickle-flavored chips or the same middle name creates an ever-so-slight affinity for the other person. In this vein, fun activities that help people make connections with their colleagues helps to build overall workplace cohesiveness.

But even the most fun team-building events and traditions, no matter how often they occur, can only do so much. In fact, they will accomplish very little in the absence of a strong culture that values communication, respect and trust. But injecting more humor and fun events into the workplace *in tandem with an inspiring culture* can do wonders to unite teams, break down barriers, help employees connect at a personal level and build the kind of inspiring culture where employees remain loyal and committed to their organization.

Here are a few more ways to focus in on this worthwhile goal:

### Family Open Houses

Hold an open house where family members are invited to tour your workplace, meet colleagues, hear presentations, view exhibits and take part in fun team activities. This is a simple but effective way to bridge the divide between employees' work lives and their personal lives and for employees to connect with the families of colleagues. Seeing a co-worker as a parent for the first time (or conversely as a child if you celebrate "Bring Your Parents to Work Day") helps you see them as real human beings first, professionals second.

### Getting to Know You Scavenger Hunts

Not just a great idea for new employees: A "get to know your colleagues scavenger hunt"—where employees seek out offbeat personal details about each other—is a great way to connect. You can create a highly customized list that encourages people to seek out very specific predetermined attributes that employees submit to the organizer. For example, Jennifer in marketing once worked for Cirque du Soleil, so one of the quest items becomes "Find someone who once hung out, literally, with Cirque du Soleil." Or create a more generic list: Find seven employees who have had unusual past hobbies or jobs; four employees who can wiggle their ears; three employees who can do a celebrity impersonation....

### Name Tags (But Not Just Any Name Tags)

This can easily be turned into a weekly tradition, wherein every Friday everyone wears a name tag that answers the question of the week: What's your favorite song? Favorite comedy? Where were you born? Cat or dog person? Favorite word? Favorite spice? Favorite Spice Girl?

### Video Bios

Kira Talent is a software company that offers a platform for companies to interview candidates via video. Many companies prefer this approach over a paper application because they get a better feel for the candidate. With a similar goal in mind, create a one-minute bio video for every new employee where they can introduce themselves to the rest of the team through a fun video message.

### Unconventional Clubs

Some workplaces have baseball teams, but what about a reading club, chess club, board game club, hiking club, birding club, fly-tying club, or gourmet cooking club?

### Job Swap Days

As the old saying goes: "Before you criticize someone, you should walk a mile in that person's shoes. That way, when you criticize him you're a mile away and you have his shoes." Or better yet, if you want to reduce silos, then creating formalized job swaps or job-shadowing days is a great first step.

### Lunch Clubs

Fun Mobility Inc. pays for employees who don't know each other to go for lunch together as a simple way to facilitate personal connections.

### Boot Camps

One of the side benefits of Zappos' month-long, hyper-intensive training program for new recruits is that it forges bonds between employees who will end up working in different departments.

### Personalized Organizational Charts

If your company has an organizational chart, put some personality and life into it by including fun photos, alter-ego job titles and interesting personal trivia.

### Meet the Employee of the Week

Send out a weekly email introducing or reintroducing an employee to everyone. Include personal, fun photos and some interesting personal trivia.

### Employee Interviews with Your Ace Reporter

Assign someone known for their humor to play the role of roving reporter by periodically interviewing employees on video about their personal and work life. Keep it light by asking quirky questions.

### Employee Interviews with Your Junior Ace Reporters

Same idea as above, but imagine how much fun it would be to have children interview the CEO and senior leaders, or to have employees' children interview their mom or dad?

**Team Commercials**
Have every team create a funny five-minute video explaining who they are and what they do. Offer a fun prize for the most creative or funniest video.

**Celebrate Your Name Week**
The first week in March is dedicated to celebrating people's names. Each day has a different theme including: Name Tag Day, Namesake Day, Name Fun Facts Day, Unique Names Day, Learn What Your Name Means Day, Middle Name Pride Day and Genealogy Day. Celebrating this week is a great way to get to know people.

**Rig Your Computers**
When a Zappos' employee logs on to their intranet site, employees play a quick round of the Face Game: A photo of a randomly selected employee pops up and the person logging in must try to correctly identify him or her and indicate whether or not they know that employee. The employee's real name and bio blurb then pops up. It's a quick and fun way to help employees learn a bit about a person who doesn't work on their immediate team.

**Why I Work Here Wall**
Create a wall dedicated to celebrating employees' dreams and personal passions. It might be a montage of images connected to people's families, a trip of a lifetime, that sailboat they are saving up to buy, or a charity they are passionate about. The point is threefold: It's a way to get to know each other's aspirations, a fun way to connect people to a sense of purpose and a way to remind them that work goes beyond a paycheck.

As you can see, there's no shortage of fun ways to help teammates get to know each other better. But you need to be intentional about it and to recognize that it's an investment in the future of your company, an investment that will pay dividends through improved communication, more respect and increased trust.

## CAN ONE PERSON MAKE A DIFFERENCE TO THE CULTURE?

The goal of all these ideas is to build a thriving culture that attracts and retains top talent, supports cohesive teamwork and collegiality and drives business growth. Naturally, the focus is on building supportive, cohesive teams. But sometimes an individual employee can have a disproportionate impact on a team, occasionally for the worst... but often for the better.

A study reported in the *International Journal of Humor Research* looked at the role of "the joker" in three different IT companies in New Zealand.[16] The study found that office jokers were considered invaluable members of their organizations by their peers and managers, playing four key roles: They pushed the boundaries; they questioned authority without subverting it; they helped develop a strong culture; and they provided much-needed stress relief. The jokers in these companies also played a key role in keeping the corporate history alive by retelling funny past stories.

Encouraging the office joker is, admittedly, a bit of a risk. But consider what a senior manager in the study had to say about the joker's role in their organization: "They are the glue of the organization and 95% of the time they are good for the company. The other 5% of the time they might overstep the mark, but overall, the good definitely outweighs the bad."

Not a bad quote to end this chapter on, for two reasons. First, all these ideas are essentially about strengthening your organizational glue so you attract and keep great employees who want to stick around your workplace *and* to each other.

The second reason this quote resonates is that when discussing any of these fun ideas—especially the ones that might be pushing the boundaries in your workplace culture—it's important to keep that perspective in mind. Not every idea will work. There might be the occasional step over the line, where you try something new that involves jump-starting people's passions. But given the potentially enormous positive impact on your organization and the potential costs of doing absolutely zilch to shake things up, the good most *definitely* outweighs the bad.

## Key Messages and Ideas

1. It's not good enough to attract the right employees. You need to be intentional about building a culture that supports their happiness and well-being and that makes them want to stick around for a while.

2. The job of retaining employees starts on day one. Making a good first impression is critical and making new employees feel like they are part of your team is essential to maintaining a strong culture.
3. The cost associated with replacing employees is bigger than you think. Investing in your culture is an insurance policy for your future. Yes, you'll still lose employees who will move onto greener pastures for the money or career opportunities. But the key to success is to make sure you aren't losing employees for the wrong reasons.
4. Happy employees are more creative and productive. Investing in employees' happiness will impact your bottom-line results.
5. Building a tribal culture helps reduce silos and barriers between teams and departments.
6. Fun traditions and rituals are critical to building a strong culture. Traditions and rituals create a sense of shared history and give employees something to look forward to and reminisce about.
7. A key way to strengthen your culture, build team cohesiveness and improve trust at work is by facilitating opportunities for employees to get to know each other beyond their job titles.

# 4

# Trumpeting Success at Work

"When purpose and fun intersect, amazing things can happen."
– Michael Kerr

Ignoring the proverbial elephant in the room can create a lot of tension in many workplaces. But at The Kjaer Group, a Danish auto parts company, it's rather hard to ignore the elephant in the room because, well, there's an actual elephant in the room. It's a stuffed toy elephant that's used to pass along praise to fellow employees who have done something worthy enough to receive the much-coveted—albeit a little silly—"Order of the Elephant."

According to the late Renn Zaphiropoulos, the former CEO of the Silicon Valley company Versatec, "*Everybody* should have an elephant." By that he meant everyone should have an elephant-sized amount of enthusiasm for their work and an elephant sized amount of recognition for what they do at work. True to his words, Zaphiropoulos once donned a satin costume and rode around his company's parking lot atop an elephant while the Stanford University marching band played alongside. He used this occasion to champion their impressive financial results and to pass out bonus checks, backing up yet another one of his beliefs: "If you're going to give someone a check, don't just mail it. Have a celebration!"

High-performing organizations understand the importance of building a culture of continual celebration, recognition and praise. Thanking people on a regular basis is one of the easiest ways to boost someone's *own* level of happiness (more on that later), while numerous studies reveal a positive link between the amount of praise given between team members and the performance of the team. Moreover, survey after survey suggests that one of the top reasons employees leave a job is because they feel unappreciated.

A Human Resource Management and Watson Worldwide survey, for example, found that a whopping 88% of employees cited a lack of acknowledgment as their top workplace issue; while 70% said a lack of recognition was the key reason they left their job.

Conversely, a study reported in *Workforce Magazine* found that regular recognition is linked to higher productivity, reduced turnover and increased job satisfaction.[1] A 2013 Gallup study found that companies that recognize employees generate 27% higher profits than companies that don't invest in employee recognition.[2] A ten-year study by Adrian Gostick and Chester Elton of 200,000 managers and employees found that simply saying "thank-you" on a regular basis translated into higher profits.[3]

Which is why I like the "Order of the Elephant." Kjaer has made it simple and fun for employees to thank each other. The stuffed elephant is a visual reminder of the importance of recognizing people's efforts. It serves as a conversation starter: When an employee notices the elephant on someone's desk they'll ask what the employee did to earn the honor, which makes the recognized employee feel great and encourages conversations on the need to provide elephant-sized service at work. (Plus it's a bit safer, simpler and cleaner than going the actual elephant/marching band route.)

But before we explore other ways of recognizing employees with a spirit of fun and good humor, let's get real for a moment, like we did at the start of the book (ah... those were good times).

## MONEY ISN'T ALWAYS HONEY

The reason the Order of the Elephant and other recognition programs are critical to the success of any organization is because money is a lousy motivator, albeit with two notable exceptions: Money encourages people to look for a job when they find themselves euphemistically "between opportunities," and money encourages employees to return to work week in and week out. In other words, money puts bums into workplace seats. But to get those bums up and moving, to engage people's hearts and minds and to fuel passions, money is simply not the best motivator. As Dan Ariely, author of *Predictably Irrational: The Hidden Forces That Shape Our Decisions,* says, "Money is often the most expensive way of motivating people."[4]

Don't get me wrong, everyone (me included) would love to have more money (feel free to send a check my way anytime you wish —I'll promptly spend it with the spirit in which it was intended). If I could wave a magic wand and ensure everyone on the planet was being paid a fair wage *and* see to it that you get that 25% raise you so deserve, I would do it in a heartbeat. Alas, I don't have a magic wand. Neither do you, and chances are neither does the organization you work for.

*Of course* thousands of employees and managers jump ship to greener pastures when they get a financial offer they simply can't refuse. *Of course* organizations must remain competitive when it comes to wages and benefits, or they will lose some top talent.

Yet, numerous studies confirm that beyond a certain amount of money—enough to sustain ourselves without worry—money has only a modest impact on people's overall levels of happiness. Homo sapiens, it turns out, tend to overestimate the impact money will have on their well-being and happiness. Some studies have even found a negative correlation between more money and overall well-being. A study reported in the *Journal of Applied Psychology* found that many people who make higher-than-average salaries feel more stressed and more time-pressured than people earning lower incomes.[5]

The research also suggests that money can have a dampening effect on creativity. Although financial bonuses can help motivate people when they are doing routine-oriented, time-pressured tasks such as stuffing envelopes or connecting widgets, studies show there is an inverse relationship when it's work that requires a high degree of creativity. People are intrinsically motivated to be creative and adding an external reward such as money appears to smother that natural tendency to create.

We also tend to overestimate the positive impact of a healthy raise due to the phenomenon known as "the hedonic treadmill:" Our expectations and desires rise in tandem with higher levels of income, resulting in no net gain in overall happiness. Moreover, within a few months that raise becomes the new norm and once that happens, it suddenly doesn't feel like it's quite enough anymore. Cue the rat race to the highest speed on the hedonic treadmill.

Again, just so we're crystal clear: Yes, I still want your boss to give you that raise because you deserve it and you've worked hard for it (I'm going out on a limb here for you now, so don't let me down).

I'm simply reminding you that if at an individual level *all you focus on* at work is the paycheck, you are likely never going to be as happy, fulfilled and motivated in your work as you might otherwise be.

If organizations focus only on the level of pay and other tangible financial incentives and ignore the elephant-sized cultural issues in their workplaces, they will never be as successful as they might otherwise be.

Companies that aspire to greatness need to do two things as it pertains to pay:

1. Do the right thing and pay people fairly. (Or better still, pay employees a *little more* than fairly.)
2. Create a purpose-driven, inspiring, passionate and fun culture that truly respects and values people so that everyone forgets they are there just to earn a paycheck.

As Mary Kay Ash of Mary Kay Cosmetics said many pink Cadillacs ago: "There are two things people want more than sex and money—recognition and praise!" (Okay, and maybe a pink Cadillac.) Which means Cuba Gooding Jr. had it only partially right in the movie *Jerry McGuire*. What he should have said is: "Show me the money, Jerry... and show me the love, Jerry! Show me the *love*!"

Which, of course, is what our hero Tom Cruise/Jerry McGuire learns through the course of the movie, thus proving my whole point.

## SHOW ME THE LOVE... MACHINE?

Philip Rosedale, the former CEO of Linden Labs (creator of the virtual world "Second Life"), used some unconventional methods to engage employees and boost happiness levels at work, including an internal software platform known as the LoveMachine. Many employees at Linden Labs work in those dreaded silos and because they often feel unconnected and unappreciated, the LoveMachine allows employees to send notes of appreciation to fellow employees which everyone could view.

You don't have to necessarily build your own love machine, but you do need to fuel your cultural engine with passion, appreciation and recognition, because intrinsic motivators such as pride will, over the long haul, almost always trump external motivators like money.

As I reminded you earlier, there's a difference between long-term employees and truly loyal employees. There's a difference between just showing up *at* work and showing up *to* work. There's a world of difference between being merely satisfied in your work and being passionately inspired to do your best work and to care deeply about the future of your company and the people around you.

But before I talk about what it takes to fire up you and your fellow troops, I have one more word of caution (the first one being that the Beatles were right, money really can't buy you love): More than being worried about motivating employees, you need to *stop de-motivating* them.

Assuming you've hired people that are already highly motivated with an amazing attitude, do you really think these self-starters need a lot of motivation? To be wildly successful, here's the Reader's Digest version of what companies need to do:

1. Hire the right people with the right attitude;
2. Give employees the training and the tools to do their jobs exceptionally well;
3. Give employees a clear sense of direction with crystal clear goals and milestones;
4. Get out of their damn way!

It's that last item—getting out of the way—that a lot of managers and companies have trouble with. Hence the need to stop de-motivating the troops. There are many things at work that inadvertently de-motivate employees: Excessive bureaucracy, micromanaging bosses, too many meetings, too many processes, a lack of true empowerment, jargon-laced communication... all of which can dampen employees' ambitions and make it that much harder for them to drag their butts out of bed on a Monday morning. These "off switches" must be identified and eliminated—or at least minimized—to successfully unshackle employees' spirits.

But merely removing the barriers to success is only part of the equation. Companies need to create an environment where people feel motivated and if not motivated, then at least inspired.

That's why inspiring organizations don't just flip the off switches; they also relentlessly strive to turn everyone on. (Okay, perhaps I could have phrased that differently.)

## SIX POWERFUL Ps OF MOTIVATION (YES, PLAY IS ONE OF THEM)

**1. Purpose**—GSD & M, an advertising agency based in Austin, Texas believes a sense of purpose at work is so important that they have a manager whose job title is "Chief Purposologist." The supermarket chain Whole Foods also understands the importance of defining a powerful purpose. Rather than the usual "blah blah blah" vision and mission statements, Whole Foods created a detailed "Declaration of Interdependence" to help employees understand why their work matters. The Declaration even includes an admission that they won't always get things right: "It is our dissatisfaction with the current reality, when compared with what is possible, that spurs us toward excellence and toward creating a better person, company, and world."

As we touched on earlier, a compelling sense of purpose is highly motivating. People crave a sense of meaning in their work lives like never before, so employees need to understand why their job matters and how it fits into the bigger picture of an organization. The greater the sense of purpose, the more employees will care about their work and the easier it will be for them to embrace change rather than fear it. You don't need to be searching for a cure for cancer or trying to solve world hunger to derive a sense of purpose from work. In fact, employing the humor advantage and tapping into a spirit of fun can help redefine a sense of purpose in many jobs.

Pike's Place fish market in Seattle, Washington has become world famous owing to their penchant for fun, most famously demonstrated through their humorous engagement with customers that often involves throwing fish madly about their fish shop, hence the "Beware of Flying Fish" signs at the shop.

So how did Pike's Place fish market become world famous? They decided to become world famous. (Aren't you glad you asked?) Seriously, that's it. They redefined their sense of purpose by creating an enormous, exciting goal that gave everyone working there a new-found sense of purpose: Rather than just working for a fish market, they now worked for a soon-to-be *world famous* fish market.

Instead of simply providing "good customer service," Pike's employees were instead challenged to "make everyone's day." Making a customer's day, I'd suggest, is a far more powerful, far more purpose-driven goal than simply providing great service. Making someone's day evokes a different mindset and opens up infinite possibilities for employees to engage with customers in a more meaningful and fun manner.

In a similar way, several children's hospitals around the world have redefined a sense of purpose for their window washers by having them dress in superhero costumes. Imagine how fun it must be for a sick ten-year-old to see Spiderman or Batman hanging outside his or her window? From the window washers' perspective, a momentous shift in their sense of purpose has taken place, from being someone whose only task is to wash the windows to someone who helps a sick child have a memorable, more fun day; from being a window washer to becoming part of a team that is helping to heal a child.

When purpose and fun intersect, amazing things can happen.

**2. Passion**—The novelist E.M. Forster once said, "I'd rather have one person who is passionate than forty people who are merely interested." Haven't we all been influenced by someone's passion? Imagine what can happen when a strong sense of purpose is fueled with passion?

Passion may sound like a vague concept, yet I've never met a successful leader who didn't talk about the role of passion in their organization and who didn't exude passion about their organization and employees. When you walk through a successful organization, you can tell instantly how passionate people are about their work. You can feel it. You can see it in how people walk, carry themselves and carry on conversations.

Gary Hamel, author of *The Future of Management*, also believes passion is one of the keys to success. Hamel suggests that when it comes to value creation in the workplace, the relative contribution of different capabilities might look something like: Passion - 35%; creativity - 25%; initiative - 20%; intellect - 15%; and diligence - 5%.

This is why organizations such as Google and 3M have found great success and unleashed innovative ideas by allowing employees a certain percentage of their time to pursue their own projects at work based on where their passions lie. Similarly, W.L. Gore, the maker of GORE-TEX®, lets its employees lead speculative new projects... as long as they are passionate about the project and they can attract enough followers.

Another way organizations are upping the passion in their workplace is by tapping into their employees' off-hour pursuits. Suppose, for example, you have an employee who loves playing piano in their off hours. Why not place a piano in your lobby or cafeteria, as one company has done, where the employee can entertain their colleagues over lunch, coffee breaks, or for special events? The employee gets to fuel their personal fire at work while contributing to a better working environment for their colleagues.

Or imagine an employee who has a passion for fitness. Why not encourage that employee to create a fitness club in their workplace as a way of promoting health and wellness at work? With a little creativity, any personal passion (okay, *almost* any) can be leveraged.

**3. Progress—** The concept of championing and celebrating small wins at work is a critical key to success. Small wins can have a disproportionate amount of power and influence beyond the achievement they represent. Yet, in one survey of senior leaders, 95% of the respondents listed "supporting progress" as the *least* important motivator at work, contrary to what all the research suggests!

Teresa Amabile and Steven Kramer, authors of *The Progress Principle,* believe that a sense of progress at work has an enormous bearing on employees' happiness and engagement levels.[7] Their research found that 76% of the time employees reported being in their best moods on days when they made progress in their jobs, whereas their worst days were the mirror image. They could find no other factors that influenced moods and happiness levels as strongly as the level of progress.

Patrick Lencioni, author of *The Three Signs of a Miserable Job,* suggests that one sign is a lack of ability to measure progress at work.[8] The other two signs are irrelevancy (not having your work tied to a sense of purpose) and anonymity (not having anyone at work know you as a real human being).

Researchers Richard Hackman and Gregory Oldman also found that the most effective form of feedback is based on progress *from the work itself*: Gardeners get feedback from the garden as it grows; computer programmers get immediate feedback when debugging computer programs; comedians get immediate feedback from their audiences.[9]

If a person has no way of knowing how they are doing, even when it is something they love to do, they will eventually lose interest. If you have no sense of progress in your work, then work can begin to feel like the movie *Groundhog Day*—an endless cycle of the same old, same old, with no end in sight.

Recognizing and supporting progress touches on a number of workplace themes: The need for timely feedback; learning new skills; goals that can be measured; removing "jobstacles" (work-related obstacles that get in the way of progress); and celebrating small wins to build momentum at work.

This last point is where a spirit of humor can help. Recognizing employees' accomplishments and celebrating milestones on their journey in fun, even outrageously elephant-sized ways, is not only a great way to build a positive culture at work, but a *necessary* means of keeping forward momentum alive.

**4. Pride**—A study by the HR service company Kenexa found that turnover rates among managers who have pride in their organizations are 21% lower than with managers who feel no pride.[10] Pride is clearly one of the most powerful intrinsic motivators. This not only comprises pride in one's own accomplishments, but also in the overall mission of an organization, team accomplishments and the products or services a company provides.

Pride is undoubtedly one of the forces Commander Abrashoff tapped into when he turned the USS Benfold's culture around. When a crew member did something noteworthy, Commander Abrashoff sent a handwritten note of appreciation, not just to the employee, but to the employee's family. Imagine a nineteen-year-old away from home for the first time and working in a challenging environment whose parents receive a positive letter from the commanding officer....

As we'll shortly discover, there are numerous means of tapping into pride at work, but one of the easiest ways is to encourage a culture of praise and recognition. It needn't come in the form of a stuffed elephant: A simple "thanks" for a job well done is what so many people crave and yet so few receive.

For praise to be truly effective and meaningful, however, it should:

- **Be sincere**—Most people can tell when you aren't being sincere, so show that you mean it and that you're not just going through the motions;
- **Be specific**—Just as when giving constructive feedback, people need to hear specifically what it is they did so well;
- **Be timely**—Effective praise comes with an expiry date, or at least it should;
- **Be 100% positive**—Avoid but-headed thinking: "Thanks for doing that for me, Sally, but next time...." All Sally will remember is, *"but next time...."*

A host of studies have focused on what constitutes effective praise. According to Dr. Carol Dweck, a social psychology professor at Stanford University, people develop and learn from setbacks and failures in two very distinct ways.[11] Some people hold what's known as a "fixed mindset belief"—that most of their abilities and intelligence levels are more or less set in stone. These people tend to perceive setbacks as a threat to their identity and sense of worth and they tend to focus on external validation.

Conversely, other people possess a "growth mindset belief"—that their abilities and intelligence can be nurtured, so they view setbacks as opportunities for growth and hence tend to be more persistent when the going gets rough.

So how does this relate to praise and motivation? Studies suggest that the best approach for nurturing growth is to praise a person's effort, not their innate talent or intelligence. A review of 150 praise studies by scholars at Stanford and Reed College support the findings that praising ability, although an ego-booster for sure, actually *reduces* persistence.[12] Conversely, praising a person's effort, their ability to grow, learn and to be challenged, their ability to deal with setbacks and praising *the process* a person goes through leads them to growth mindset behaviors, where they view setbacks as challenges to overcome and mere speed bumps on the road to success.

Of course, the icing on the praise cake happens when you add a bit of fun into the mix. Saying thank-you is great. Saying thank-you with a stuffed elephant is great *and* memorable.

**5. Play**—The question at the heart of the experiment was this: Would Stockholm subway riders choose the stairs over the escalator if it was more fun to do so? By installing a musical piano staircase, 66% more people did indeed opt for the stairs. This experiment was part of Volkswagen's "Fun Theory" contest, wherein people submitted ideas suggesting how behaviors could be changed by making it fun. The contest came out of Volkswagen's belief that if they could make it fun for people to drive environmentally friendly cars, more people would do so. The winning submission in the Fun Theory contest was an idea for a photo radar lottery where people driving under the speed limit would be entered into a draw from the funds amassed through the speeders.

The Fun Theory isn't rocket science. It's about tapping into every person's innate desire to play and have fun. It's simply recognizing that when work feels like play, it doesn't feel so much like work anymore. To quote a mantra from Integris Credit Union, "Work made fun, gets done!" Play makes time pass quicker. Play truly is the sugar with the cough syrup that can help anything go down just a wee bit smoother.

One way to tap into the power of play at work is to turn desired behaviors into a game. Zingerman's Roadhouse restaurant in Ann Arbor, Michigan, for example, improved their customer service scores considerably after creating a "greeter game" wherein the host team was challenged to greet every seated patron within five minutes. Other games involved incentives for the fewest knife injuries in the kitchen, neatest kitchens and fewest returned meals.

Don't dismiss the notion of play as something trivial. Milliken, a global design and manufacturing company, with thirty-nine manufacturing facilities throughout the world, is a company that can lay claim to being not only a global leader in innovation and design, but also to being one of the most inspiring workplaces I have ever visited. In 2012 Milliken celebrated its sixth consecutive year of recognition by *Ethisphere Magazine* in its "World's Most Ethical Companies" list. Their focus on doing good is ingrained in their history and runs deep through their culture. Milliken's recycling program, for example, predates most company recycling programs not by years, but by *decades*, having started in, wait for it... 1900! Throughout the depression, Milliken helped to keep many small towns in the United States alive. They've helped communities in times of crisis and today their sustainability practices are decades ahead of the marketplace. Part of their innovative practice is their workplace creed which embodies a concept they call Purposeful Play.[13]

Purposeful Play is the spirit with which Milliken employees embrace their work. It's about playing with passion, with a sense of purpose and with imagination to achieve success. It's a mindset to describe how employees seek out opportunities, explore challenges and work toward creating a better world through unique insights and innovative designs.

**6. Personal—**A study from Newcastle University found that cows treated with a personal touch, such as being given their own unique name, produced as much as 285 more liters of milk per year![14] If it works with cows, I'm guessing there's a reasonably good chance that the personal touch works with humans as well.

When it comes to motivating people, however, I'd suggest you forget the golden rule of "treating everyone the way you'd like to be treated," because the reality is that some people don't want to be treated the way you want to be treated. Instead, think "different strokes for different folks." To be truly successful you need to find the individual triggers, the off and on switches for every employee on your team. Organizations need to treat people individually and recognize that every person has a unique set of challenges, fears, hopes and dreams.

Consider a survey from Dogster.com which found that 49% of dog owners would switch jobs tomorrow if they could bring their dog to work with them; 66% would work longer hours and 33% would take a cut in pay in lieu of being able to bring Fido along to the office. My point here isn't that you should make your workplace dog-friendly (though more and more workplaces are finding positive results in terms of reduced stress levels and higher morale by doing just that). My point is that who would have imagined that for some people, bringing their dogs to work with them is such a huge factor in their overall happiness.

So leaders need to have regular conversations with their employees about what inspires them and what turns them off, about what gives them a sense of purpose in their work, how they want their progress to be measured, what makes them proud and how they like to play. The answers may be slightly different for every person. Or they might be monumentally different. Susan might love to be thanked publically, whereas Dan dreads the notion of a public ceremony. Bob might truly appreciate a free golf membership whereas Kelly views it as her worst nightmare. Jenny derives a sense of purpose when she is able to help a customer in a meaningful way, whereas Hal's sense of purpose comes from knowing the company is being a good environmental steward.

Employees also need to take the initiative and start these conversations, even if at first just with themselves. After all, when was the last time *you* seriously reflected on what you want and don't want out of your work?

## JOB, CAREER, OR CALLING?

There's no getting around the fact that attitude drives success at work, starting with how you view your job. Yale researcher Amy Wrzesniewski studied how our mental conceptions of work affect performance.[15] She found that people fall into one of three broad categories in terms of how they define their work: A job, a career, or a calling. The "job folks" view work as only a means to an end—it's all about paying the bills. Those with a "career orientation" are more likely to be focused on success and looking for long-term advancement, but ultimately still view work as a means to an end. The final group, with the "calling orientation," tend to love their work for the sake of the work itself, not just because of the external rewards.

Wrzesniewski's research found that in one sample of administrative assistants, the group divided out almost evenly into each of those three categories, despite the similar nature of their work. She has found doctors who view their work simply as a job and front-line employees who view their work as a calling. The key finding in her research is that our attitude about the nature of our work affects performance: Those people who view their work as a calling tend to be happier and more fulfilled and to experience greater success in the workplace.

So an important question to ask when it comes to recognizing employees and creating an environment that inspires and motivates people is this: Are all of your efforts helping employees move away from a job mindset toward a purpose-driven, passionate *calling*?

## PUTTING ON YOUR BEST FORMAL

Anyone can learn the names of their employees or customers, but how many people take the time to learn the names of their customers' dogs? I met a salesperson once who not only learned the names of his key clients' dogs, but also sent birthday greetings on the dogs' birthdays! Why? Because he recognized that to his rural farming clients, dogs are valued members of the family. In other words, he wasn't just dropping names, he was demonstrating that he recognized what mattered to his customers.

Similarly in the workplace, true recognition isn't about just naming names or handing out "Employee of the Month" honors from on high. Eons ago when I worked as a manager, I received a special award from on high. Of course I was honored. I was less honored, however, when the award was given to me by someone who I'd never met before and for something *other* than what I thought I was receiving the honor for!

More formal workplace recognition programs definitely have their place, but that place should occupy a lower rung on the recognition ladder. Nothing is more important, or as valuable, as the day-to-day recognition efforts that must be built into the fiber of your workplace culture. And if you have formal recognition programs of any kind, make them as meaningful and as valuable as possible.

Here are some key questions to answer before recognizing someone in your workplace:

### Who?

Who would the person most appreciate receiving the honor from? Perhaps it's a colleague, an employee, the entire team, a valued customer, or even a family member. Being given the honor from the person who most understands what the award means will have the biggest impact on the individual receiving it.

### What?

What does the honoree truly value? What are their personal passions or charity interests? Are they receiving something they will truly value and appreciate? Can you contact an employee's family member for input? (Incidentally, although surveys show that employees say they would prefer to have cash bonuses, studies and follow-up surveys reveal that gifts, especially those involving experiences, are more meaningful and memorable.)

**When and Where?**

Is the honor being bestowed in a timely enough fashion to be meaningful and in a location that is special to the person?

**Why?**

Does everyone understand the rationale for the honor and how it links to your team's success and the overall purpose of your organization?

**How?**

Is the honor being bestowed in a manner that the person will appreciate? Some employees will revel in a public parade, but many might be horrified at the prospect, so make sure you really understand the tone the person would most appreciate: Private or public? Understated or overstated? Disco-themed rollerblading bash or British-style tea and crumpets?

Remember, recognizing employees isn't always about what's convenient for the company or what's worked in the past for other employees, it's about *what's best for the person being honored.* And although this may seem obvious, it's important to have fun! I've sat through many awards ceremonies that felt overly somber. So remember that even though it may be more formal, it's still a celebration!

## FUELING AN ATTITUDE OF GRATITUDE AT WORK

There's a selfish reason to promote a workplace environment of recognition and appreciation: Studies suggest that it's not just the people who get thanked (the thankees?) who feel better, the thankers have much to be thankful for as well.

In his book, *Thanks,* Dr. Robert A. Emmons details how his research found that people who expressed sincere gratitude over a ten-week period (by maintaining a gratitude journal) felt 25% happier than people who didn't maintain the journal.[16] They were also more optimistic about the future, felt better about their lives and did 1.5 hours more exercise a week than people who focused on the things that went wrong each day.

Researchers at the University of California showed that "grateful people report higher levels of positive emotions, life satisfaction, vitality and optimism and lower levels of depression and stress."[17] In fact, dozens of separate studies from around the world confirm the benefits of expressing gratitude not just to ourselves, but especially to those around us.

The studies found that expressing gratitude to other people plays a significant role in social bonding. Frequent opportunities to express gratitude lead to increased well-being, better health, better exercise habits, higher life satisfaction and increased optimism. Even just a one-time act of thoughtful gratitude was found to produce an immediate 10% increase in happiness.

A study out of Brigham Young University in Utah also found that you can significantly boost your level of happiness for up to four weeks when you *share* positive news with supportive people.[18] The happiness boost was found to exceed the typical boost a person receives from reliving an event and much greater than one receives from simply writing down the great news. The study also found that people who impart good news at least twice a week to a supportive person report greater overall life satisfaction.

Yet again, there's a chicken-and-egg relationship involving humor. The more grateful people are, the happier they tend to be, making it easier for them to find the humor in their lives. Conversely, tapping into our sense of humor as a way to maintain a positive and supportive attitude tends to make people more willing to show their gratitude and be more generous to the people around them.

## BUILDING A CULTURE OF RECOGNITION AND APPRECIATION

Hal Rosenbluth, CEO of the corporate travel agency Rosenbluth International, wrote a book that sums up the secret to their phenomenal success: *The Customer Comes Second: Put Your People First and Watch 'em Kick Butt.*[19] The somewhat counterintuitive approach of putting the customer second was an intentional decision by Rosenbluth, one that paid off in spades.

It's a great reminder that for recognition to be truly effective at work, it has to be ingrained in the culture and it needs to start at the top. All the fun traditions and rewards in the world won't work unless employees genuinely feel valued and indeed, feel as though they are the company's #1 priority.

Here's an interesting exercise to try: Have all your employees fill in the end of this sentence: "My organization puts ___________ first, above all else." (What answers might you get? Profits... process... politics... safety... the environment... people? It might be worthwhile finding out.)

There are hundreds of ways to recognize employees and demonstrate that we appreciate them. Incidentally, by employees I mean managers as well—it's just as important that they feel the love too and not just every October 16th, on official "Boss Day."

We show that we appreciate people when we ask about their weekends and their families, when we show an interest in their work goals and challenges, when we allow them greater responsibilities and more freedom, when we offer them more challenging assignments, when we take a moment to sincerely thank them, when we offer up some genuine praise and when we ask them for their input.

A survey by Marshall Goldsmith and Associates found that the #1 thing employees said they wanted more of at work was to be asked for input.[20] When we ask someone at work for input, it sends the message that we value their experience, wisdom and judgment. It's one of the simplest things we can do to engage people's hearts and minds and yet surveys suggest it's the thing managers most frequently fail to do.

Asking for input, praising people and expressing sincere thanks is largely a matter of habit. It's also about building the kind of culture that champions these attitudes and behaviors, which again loops us back to the importance of fun traditions and rituals. Traditions built around recognizing people and celebrating their accomplishments and milestones helps build momentum and reminds everyone of the need to make this a way of life. It could be as simple as creating a ritual to start each meeting by having everyone go around the table and take a moment to sincerely thank or praise someone.

There are hundreds of excellent resources on recognizing employees (Bob Nelson's book, *1001 Ways to Reward Employees,* is one of them). But since we're talking about the humor advantage, I want to highlight some of the more fun and offbeat ways to celebrate success and recognize employees.

***Offer Recognition for Offbeat Reasons***

- Celebrate the founding date of your company.
- Celebrate the anniversary of when employees started working for you.
- Celebrate your fiscal new year.
- Create and celebrate everyone's work-related New Year's resolutions.
- Create a highlights video, scrap book, or yearbook of the top achievements for the previous year or create a top-ten highlights ceremony to remind everyone how much has been accomplished.
- Hershey Foods has a special award, "The Exalted Order of the Extended Neck," to reward people who buck the system. Similarly, Biogen Idec Canada has an employee-nominated "Take the Bull by the Horns" award, which is given out at each of their town hall meetings to an employee who embodies the company culture by challenging the status quo.
- An annual World Pizza Games competition includes events such as the pizza triathlon, fastest box folding, fastest dough, largest dough and individual acrobatic dough making. Hey, if pizza making can be turned into a competitive event, then *anything* in your workplace can be turned into a fun competitive event. (And I mean, anything: There's a phenomenon known as "Extreme Accounting" where accountants take their work to extreme locations—mountaintops, sea beds, roller coaster rides or skydiving.)
- There's a Pizza Hall of Fame, so why not a _________ Hall of Fame?

***Offer Offbeat Rewards***

- Depending on where your offices are, allow employees one "snow day," "surf's up day" or "sun's out day" per year where they can sneak out for the afternoon to take advantage of the weather.

- To help employees celebrate their birthdays, create a policy where they are allowed to leave work two hours early on their birthday and/or arrive two hours late the day after (when, in fact, it may be even more appreciated).
- Hold a Limo Lottery, where the winning employee gets dropped off to work and picked up again by a limo.
- Alpine Tubular Management & Supply Inc. hands out a trophy made from a golden upside down toilet plunger holding some fake "poop" once a month to an employee or team that "gives a crap" by going above and beyond the call of duty.
- Zappos has a program to recognize workplace heroes. As part of its Hero Award program, each employee is given a $50 monthly allowance to award a colleague as a bonus. The executive team then picks an overall hero from all the candidates. The winning workplace hero is announced with a mini-parade while a song such as "I Need a Hero" plays on the office sound system. The hero of the month gets a special parking space for a month, a $150 Zappos gift card and, as befitting any true hero, a cape.
- Rogers Insurance in Calgary, Alberta rewards employees through their "Dream Program" which allows all employees to register their dream wishes. Then, each year, four employees (one selected anonymously by a staff vote, one anonymously by management and two by random draws) receive $10,000 toward achieving their dream. The company also adds $100 a year into each employee's "Dream Account," from which they can withdraw money at any time to put toward their dreams and gives an additional $1,000 dream stipend to one randomly selected employee.
- Cable & Wireless Optus in Sydney, Australia held a lottery to name floors in their building after employees. The winning employee gets the floor officially named for them, complete with a plaque and photo on the associated wall.

- Hold a *Ferris Bueller's Day Off* contest, wherein employees submit their ideas for what they'd do for the day if they could play hooky. The winner (either through a draw or a vote for the most creative idea) gets the chance to live their dream hooky day.
- A Wells Fargo office in California has a list of 101 awards and prizes, including some rather offbeat ones such as hot air ballooning, getting your house cleaned, music lessons for your child and a complete personal makeover.
- Have a "celebrity for the day" contest where the winner gets the full celeb treatment, complete with limo, paparazzi and glamour photo shots.
- Make a donation to the employee's charity of choice to honor them on their birthday.

***Offer Recognition to Off-the-Beaten-Path People***

- The third Friday of December is official Underdog Day to recognize unsung heroes that don't typically get noticed. But don't wait until December, create a list of the unsung heroes in your workplace and plan some fun events and awards to honor them on a regular basis.
- Don't just recognize individuals. If you want to build team spirit, be sure to recognize teams as well.
- Recognize the family members of your employees for their role as supporting players. Bur-Jon Steel Service Center sends flowers and free dinner coupons to spouses or partners, along with a personal note of thanks, when employees work long stretches of overtime.
- Create rewards and recognition for your partners, vendors and suppliers.

***Celebrate in Offbeat Style***

- Create a celebrations calendar for the year that highlights everyone's birthday, anniversary date, significant social events and milestones.
- During their busiest times of the year, executives at the insurance company the Cigna Group push coffee carts

through the office, serving drinks and goodies to front-line employees as a way to recognize their efforts and to connect with them.

- Employees at Atlanta-based Corporate Resource Development set off a siren every time they achieve a major sale.
- Create a spoof Academy Awards ceremony.
- Have everyone's egos massaged. Everyone gets five minutes in a comfy chair while someone massages their ego, flattering them profusely with how wonderful they are.
- If there isn't one already, create an official day each year to celebrate and recognize your unique profession.
- Place messages of thanks in unusual, off-the-wall locations throughout the office.
- Earn raffle ticket entries by doing something that goes above and beyond the call of duty.

To create a culture of recognition in your workplace, start slow and keep it simple... *but start!* Take heart in the fact that a study from the University of California and Harvard University has found that spreading thanks and sharing acts of kindness is highly contagious: When a person receives a gift or a kind favor, they are more likely to be generous and pass along an even bigger gift to someone else.[21] In fact, the researchers found that one good act was often the catalyst for three more acts of kindness.

So if you want your workplace to be recognized as a truly inspiring place to work, catch the bug and start a recognition epidemic today.

You can always thank me later.

### Key Messages and Ideas

1. High-performing organizations continually celebrate success and recognize employees.
2. Money is neither the most effective nor the most powerful motivational lever. Inspiring companies pay their employees fairly, but to

turn long-term employees into passionate and engaged employees, they focus on building an inspiring culture that values people.

3. Inspiring companies and inspiring leaders identify and minimize any "off switches"—practices that may be de-motivating employees.
4. Six powerfully effective motivators include: **p**urpose, **p**assion, **p**rogress, **p**ride, and **p**lay—all made **p**ersonal by recognizing an individual's specific needs.
5. Inspiring workplaces strive to create an environment where people shift from a "job" mentality to a "calling" mindset.
6. For formal recognition programs to be effective, focus on what's best for the person receiving the honor.
7. Creating a culture of recognition and appreciation starts at the top with a relentless focus on employees as your #1 priority.
8. Get creative and inject some fun into your appreciation and recognition efforts by celebrating for offbeat reasons with offbeat rewards in offbeat style.

# 5

# To Be Contagious, Make Your Messages Outrageous

"The single biggest problem with communication is the illusion that it has taken place."

– George Bernard Shaw

"We didn't mean to make you cry. We didn't want to say good-bye. We're *so* sorry. We'll write your name across the sky. Cue the airplane guy... with a double sorry! Triple sorry! We were really super wrong...." (Feel free to chime in if you know the words.)

Rather than the usual corporate double-speak form letter: "We regret any inconvenience this may have inadvertently blah, blah, blah..." (seriously, who talks like that in the real world, anyway?), imagine an apology in the form of a customizable music video offering not just an apology, but a "*triple sorry* apology" and a confession of being "really super wrong"? How could you stay mad at someone who goes to that much effort and good humor to make amends?

The above lyrics are part of a hilariously endearing music video Johnson & Johnson created after a production glitch resulted in a shortage of one of their popular feminine hygiene products. Upon hearing how upset their customers were, Johnson & Johnson decided to make amends by creating an online music video where their female clientele could submit their first name and then have the lyrics and visuals customized specifically for them: Their name would appear written in the sand, in the sky by the "airplane guy" and even on the tattooed bicep of the cute male singer. The opening lyrics would be sung specifically to that customer. The song ends with the heartfelt lines: "You deserve the best and more... so take this coupon to the store." Wow. A song *and* a coupon. Does it get any better than that?

The video immediately went viral and earned awards and numerous accolades for its creative approach. More importantly, it worked. The video conveyed a sincere apology delivered with a heavy dose of gentle humor, without coming across as trite or sarcastic.

In other words, Johnson & Johnson scored a home run by turning the usual corporate "deja moo"—the feeling you've heard this bull before, into "deja new"—the feeling you've never seen or heard anything like this before.

Whether communicating with your customers or building an inspiring workplace culture, if you want your messages, ideas and brand to stand out from the herd to be heard, humor is one of the most potent tools in your communications arsenal.

## COMMUNICATION IS EVERYTHING

Communication in the workplace is everything and everything is communication.

Whether you're trying to instill your vision and values, recognize people and celebrate success, build a strong team, tear down silos, manage conflict, offer stellar customer service or, for that matter, add more humor to your workplace, it all comes down to communication. *Communication is everything.*

All communication begins with actions, because yes, actions really do speak louder than words and talk really is cheap (unless you live in Canada where we live with some of the most expensive mobile phone rates in the world... but I digress). The people in your organization send countless messages to each other and to your customers simply through their behaviors. So *everything is communication.*

This is why effective and inspiring communication is one of the soundest business investments you can make. Companies rated by their employees as being in the top 25% in openness of communication delivered an average shareholder return of 7.9% over a ten-year period, compared with only 2.1% at companies that ranked lower in these measures.[1] The Corporate Executive Board tracked 130 worldwide companies across seven key indicators and found that the indicator most strongly correlated with higher financial returns was the employees' comfort level in being able to speak up about any issue. Another study of more than fifty large companies by the Ferrazzi Greenlight consulting company observed that "observable candor" was *the* behavior that best predicted high-performing teams.[2]

Conversely, according to the book, *Why Business People Speak Like Idiots: A Bullfighter's Guide*, the heavy use of buzzword jargon in organizations results in lower morale and trust and leads to lost productivity.[3] Finally, a University of Carolina study found that poor workplace meetings play a substantial role in driving top talent away from organizations.

But it doesn't take an exhaustive list of studies to reach the common-sense conclusion that ineffective workplace communication generates confusion and conflict, ramps up stress, stifles creativity, divides teams, fosters a silo mentality and ultimately impacts every aspect of your business... and not for the better.

It's no wonder then that inspiring leaders and companies are intentional about their communication. Great leaders and high-performing employees don't think of communication as an afterthought or as someone else's job, they integrate it into everything they do and recognize effective communication for the investment that it is. Did the Johnson & Johnson apology video cost a bit of change? To say the least. But by turning a negative situation on its head, wowing customers and generating mountains of positive press, the video more than paid for the investment.

Of course, when it comes to communication it's not just *what* you say that matters, it's *how* you say it. So the question concerning us here is: Can humor help make your communication more effective and thus help you laugh all the way to the bank?

## A STAND-UP ECONOMIST WALKS INTO A BAR...

Speaking of banks, did you hear the one about the economist who walks into a bar... and delivers a stand-up comedy routine?

Yoram Bauman, who holds a PhD in economics, bills himself as the world's first stand-up economist. Having met him in person, I can vouch for the fact that he really is a stand-up kind of guy. But given that his hilarious YouTube video deconstructing ten principles of economics has garnered over a million hits, he clearly comes by his moniker honestly. For anyone who's ever been lulled to sleep during a macroeconomics course or dropped into a coma after trying to slog through an article on Gross Domestic Product, consider that Bauman has done the unthinkable: He's made economics fun.

In addition to his humorous talks, Bauman has produced two very funny cartoon books explaining the basic principles of micro and macroeconomics. When you get rave reviews from laypeople with no economics background *and* a Nobel Laureate in the field... you're clearly doing something right.

Do you need to fine-tune your stand-up comedy skills to inject more humor into your communication? Actually, as we'll see shortly, it's not such an off-the-wall idea. But my point for now is simply that, as Yoram Bauman, Johnson & Johnson and, as you'll recall, even the Swedish military have proven, any topic—no matter how serious, corporate, or deadly dull it might appear on the surface—can benefit from a humor injection. On a broader scale, championing a culture that values both communication and humor will help you achieve *all* your workplace goals.

## CHOOSING TO BE EFFECTIVE

Kim Axelson, CEO of AFA JCDecaux, arranged a rather outrageous stunt to make a point to his employees about effective communication in the workplace. Frustrated over their reliance on email, Axelson arranged for his IT manager to intercept everyone's internal emails and post them via good old-fashioned snail mail. A few days later, each employee received a surprise in the form of a huge pile of paper mail. Outrageous? You bet. But the point was made and the use of email in their office plunged dramatically, as employees opted to either pick up the phone or get off their duffs and talk to each other in person.

There's a big difference between efficient communication and effective communication. Of course email is a wonderfully *efficient* tool, but what Axelson understood was that it's not very effective along the way.

As someone once wisely observed, "The written word does not smile." In fact, several studies suggest emails have a big tonal issue: In almost *half* of the emails sent, the person on the receiving end isn't quite certain what the sender's intended tone was supposed to convey. This is why some organizations have purposely designed their offices to encourage more face-to-face communication, while other organizations have instituted technology-free days to encourage more personal interaction.

Small talk, "water-cooler talk," or fun socials at work aren't always viewed as an efficient use of time, but how else do employees get to know one another beyond mere job titles? How else do employees build relationships and trust unless people are connecting at a personal level? A University of Western Ontario study found that water-cooler conversations actually *do* increase productivity at work. So although small talk and social events may not appear efficient, over the long term they're highly effective.

When leaders communicate via monologues, it's highly efficient. The lack of pesky questions and other points of view tends to speed up the whole "communication" process. But real communication is never one-sided. It's an ongoing dialogue, which means effective communication is going to be time-consuming and messy and, at times, it can even create conflict.

Finally, it might be more efficient to communicate messages by sticking to bare-bones facts devoid of creativity, humanity, or humor. But is it effective? Not by a long shot.

All of these themes interconnect: The more real conversations you encourage at work, the stronger the relationships become, which leads to higher levels of trust. The stronger the trust and the more face-to-face interactions, the more apt people are to find and share humor, since humor is often a byproduct of social interactions.

Just as humor in the workplace can't be an afterthought, effective communication in the workplace requires a cultural approach. How, after all, can employees speak with candor unless there's an environment of mutual respect and trust? How can effective communication happen if leaders aren't approachable? How can real conversations take place when employees sense that style is valued over substance, or monologues championed over dialogues?

Using humor creates an atmosphere conducive to trust, because people come across as authentic human beings. Leaders who share their sense of humor convey vulnerability when they are willing to laugh at themselves and that vulnerability makes them more approachable, not to mention more likable.

Yet again, there's a chicken-and-egg relationship between an inspiring workplace culture and positive communication. The more of an upbeat, humor-filled workplace you create, the easier it is for people to communicate with each other in a positive manner... because they're happy! Conversely, the more positively people communicate with each other, the more positive the tone of the entire workplace.

## ARE YOU POSITIVE?

Research suggests that people retain negative emotions longer than positive emotions. Energy-draining culture vultures who do nothing but complain and exude constant negativity are detrimental to any workplace. After a decade of research on high- and low-performing teams, organizational psychologist and consultant Marcial Losada found that 2.9013 is the ratio of positive to negative communication necessary to make a business team successful.[4] This three-to-one ratio of positive to negative comments is known as the "Losada line." Losada's research also suggests that really high-performing teams have a ratio of positive to negative comments closer to a six-to-one ratio.

This doesn't mean everyone needs to don rose-colored glasses and live in Never-Never Land. Open candor and healthy disagreement are necessary parts of a thriving organization. Avoiding these things only leads to more conflict in the long run. An absence of conflict may reflect a lack of willingness to speak truth to power and can lead to unresolved tension in the workplace, which often translates to losing out on great ideas that might otherwise have generated untold windfalls for your business. If there's never any conflict, chances are you haven't fostered a climate of trust, respect and openness.

An aptly titled study in *Harvard Business Review*—"How Manage–ment Teams Can Have a Good Fight"—found that teams managing conflict most effectively were the ones that consistently used humor, pulled pranks and told jokes during meetings.[5]

It shouldn't be surprising to learn that conflict can be unhealthy, too. So it's important to remember that we need to nurture a climate conducive to healthy, constructive conflict where people have passionate—even heated—debates over *substance,* not personality.

If used effectively, humor can help here, too. Studies have shown that if you can get people laughing in a conflict situation, they tend to shift from thinking in a convergent manner (seeing only one possible solution) to thinking divergently (seeing that other resolutions might exist).

In some circumstances, this may even save you money. Studies into US malpractice suits found that primary care physicians who used more humor and laughter with their patients were less likely to be sued than their more staid counterparts.[6]

Even if it doesn't shift people's thinking, humor can soften an otherwise difficult or challenging message. As comedian Mary Hirsh once said, "Humor is like a rubber sword—it allows you to make a point without drawing blood." So when Gandhi was asked what he thought of western civilization, his response—"I think it would be a good idea"—softened what could have been taken as a sharp rebuke of western values. When Ronald Reagan was asked if his age was an issue during a 1984 presidential debate with challenger Walter Mondale, the president scored laughs and nullified the issue with his response: "I am not going to exploit, for political purposes, my opponent's youth and inexperience." Even Mondale laughed and the issue was never raised again during the election.

The mayor of Lanjaron, Spain passed a law prohibiting death as a satirical way of forcing the government to release more land for a new cemetery. The law became extremely popular among residents and was taken in the spirit of humor it was intended. Sure, this may not *appear* to fall under the umbrella of communication, but the actions of the mayor sent a very effective message to the government and isn't that what good communication is all about?

Which brings us back once again to the role of the joker in speaking uncomfortable truths to people in positions of power under the cover of humor. Like the court jester in ancient Egyptian or medieval times, or Jon Stewart's *Daily Show* in modern times, office jokers can play an important role in speaking truth to power. After all, as George Bernard Shaw once said: "If you're going to tell people the truth you better make them laugh. Otherwise, they'll kill you."

In medieval times the court jester was typically a trusted confidante of the royal inner circle. The royals often became tired of the false compliments and praise from their "yes men," and appreciated the honest insights jesters provided. Some royal courts even consulted jesters before going to battle. In 1386, the Duke of Austria asked his jester for an opinion on his plans to attack the Swiss. The jester reportedly said, "You fools, you're all debating how to get into the country, but none of you have thought how you're going to get out again." Point taken... without anyone losing their heads (literally).

Similarly, the Bambuti pygmies of the Congo jungles know a thing or two about using humor in difficult office situations. (Okay, maybe not so much office situations, but since everyone agrees that work is a jungle, maybe we can still learn something from them.) The Bambuti designate an official "camp clown," whose job is to diffuse any tribal interpersonal conflict. By mocking the tension or humorously taking on the blame himself through his antics, he resolves conflicts without any violence.

Yes, this tradition can easily extend to corporate environments. The former CEO of British Airways, Sir Colin Marshall, appointed Paul Birch to the position of corporate fool. Birch was given permission to speak up, challenge conventional wisdom and create a little turbulence. He helped employees approach problems in different ways and highlighted times when the company was acting, well, foolish. As Birch retells in the book, *Willful Blindness*, "The jester's role is to draw attention to things that are going wrong, to stir things up. You want to build organizations where everyone sees provocation as one of their essential roles." [7]

Anyone donning the jester's cap in the workplace may at times come across as sarcastic, perhaps even subversive, in their use of humor. But keep in mind that some people are only comfortable speaking candidly by burying their message in humor. Yes, the humor may be edgy at times and it may not be the most effective means of making a point. But wise leaders should recognize the important role workplace jesters play in communicating important—if not always welcome—messages. If these leaders are smart, they'll listen for the truth buried in the punch lines. As an old saying goes, if you want to make a point, tell a story. If you want to make several points, use humor.

Some companies leverage creative outlets such as skit nights or interactive improv presentations, where employees often reveal more honest opinions about what they really think of certain business practices or workplace issues. Risky? Maybe. But if done properly, invaluable insights can be gleaned when employees are given permission to tap into their inner jester and the audience is prepared for the truth. As the American essayist George Saunders once said, "Humor is what happens when we're told the truth quicker and more directly than we're used to."

## SIMPLY SPEAKING

Bloated workplace jargon is the buzzword bane of business banter. Jargon quite simply sucks the life out of any form of communication by giving everyone a serious case of the blah, blah, blahs. Numerous organizations post annual "Top-ten Most Annoying Buzzword" lists to highlight this irritating scourge of workplace communication. Phrases that have made frequent appearances on these lists include: "At the end of the day;" "change management;" "customer-centric;" "do more with less;" "deliverables;" "going forward;" "paradigm shift..." and hundreds more that manage to weasel their way into day-to-day business communication. Jargon is ineffective not just because it's so uninspiring and unimaginative, but because it's equally vague and meaningless.

Which is why every workplace needs a buzzword jar, where people toss a quarter into the pot each time they use a common buzzword term or overused acronym. Some workplaces hold buzzword bingo games during their meetings as a fun way to remind everyone to keep their language simple and direct. The consulting company Silver Lining Ltd. even holds a monthly "corporate speak" theme day where they purposely talk like big business hotshots using as much convoluted jargon as possible, to help remind everyone to speak plainly the rest of the time.

So to be effective and inspiring you need to speak simply. But is there ever a time when internal jargon can be a good thing?

If you've seen the Owen Wilson/Vince Vaughan comedy, *The Internship,* you may recall the use of the term "Googliness" to describe that certain hard-to-pin-down quality that Google employees seek when hiring new employees. Yes, the real-life version of Google uses the term as a fun shorthand way to describe the virtues of an ideal Google employee. And there's more: Google's California headquarters is known as the Googleplex; employees are known as Googlers; new employees are newglers; ex-Google employees are, naturally, xooglers.

Creating your own internal fun lingo (emphasis on fun) that riffs off your organization's name or key terms is a great way to add a bit of fun while strengthening your brand identity and culture. If you include the terms in your employee handbooks—or even create a dictionary or a training video on how to use the terms correctly—it might even proactively help you on a go-forward basis so that, at the end of the day, it will impact every bottom-line, customer-centric aspect of your profit center. Sorry, I meant to say, "It'll help." Especially when it comes to speaking human.

## SPEAK HUMAN

When the social media management platform Hootsuite goes into sleep mode because you haven't tweeted anything for a while, the owl icon lets you know with the message: "I was bored, so I decided to take a nap. Let me know when you get back." It sounds eerily un-owl-like... and very humanoid-like.

Or consider this example from a T-Mobile cell phone quick start guide:

- Use only batteries from the original manufacturer (hint—if it's being sold out of someone's car trunk, walk away);
- Keep your phone close—if it rings and you discover it's in the back seat, do *not* crawl over the seat to answer it while driving;
- Phones aren't cheap, so keep it in a safe place—away from children who may find it fun to see if the phone sinks or floats and away from dogs that find plastic-coated products to be irresistible chew toys.

Again, eerily humanlike, conversational and funny to boot!

But the prize for speaking conversationally with copious amounts of safe humor has to go to the deal-of-the-day website Groupon, where copy for a golf club re-gripping package opens with:

> "Shopping for golf clubs is a lot like buying a used car: always get the one that drives into the fewest trees. Drive straight and true with today's Groupon."

They even have a name for the tone they want to convey in their marketing copy—*The Groupon Voice*—and an editorial manual that lays out how to inject humor into their deal descriptions. The manual advises writers to aim for a twenty to eighty ratio of humorous to informative content, and stresses the need to use safe humor and stay away from overtly hipster tendencies.

A multiple-choice quiz helps guide new Groupon writers in the effective use of humor. For example: *The kitchen is statistically the most dangerous room in a home because it contains the highest concentration of knives, open flames and:*

a. *Cereal killers;*
b. *Spoiled fruit;*
c. *Mother-in-laws;*
d. *Pots of semi-living lobsters.*

The Groupon Voice correct answer is "d." Lobsters are quirky. But opting for the pun of cereal killers is too obvious and cutesy, while the mother-in-law response would run the risk of offending some of their customers.

The point of finding a more human voice is this: Most normal, well-functioning people don't go home on a Friday evening and fire up a PowerPoint presentation for the family or speak using convoluted buzzwords. They have conversations. They laugh and share stories. They speak human.

But speaking human isn't just about using plain, direct language. It's also about being conversational and authentic and conveying a tone that people trust. As we've seen, whether it's in help-wanted ads, job descriptions, employee manuals, safety regulations, voice mail messages, website communication, or email auto-responders, speaking human brings messages to life by imbuing them with a personality.

This isn't about being lazy, sloppy, or overly casual with your language. Nor is it about dropping the "f bomb" so you sound more real. It's simply recognizing that to be more effective and professional when you connect with other humans, it helps to sound like a living, breathing human being.

## TELL YOUR STORIES

Steve Cody, the co-founder and managing partner of New York communications agency Peppercomm, understands the power of humor and storytelling to help package his clients' messages. But as a part-time stand-up comedian, he's also a huge believer in the power of humor to change the way people interact and communicate with one another, transforming an entire workplace culture along the way.

After taking a stand-up comedy workshop and catching the comedy bug himself, Cody couldn't help but notice the many lessons that crossed over into his work life. "I realized I was becoming a better communicator, starting with my listening skills. In comedy you are trained to read body language cues from the audience, to listen intensely to the feedback and to cope with silences. So doing comedy made me a much better listener, it helped me think on my feet and it helped dramatically improve my business presentations to clients."[8]

Cody was such a comedy convert that he insisted the entire Peppercomm management team take the comedy training as well. "At first everyone balked. They couldn't see the connection to business, plus some were naturally terrified. But after doing the workshop, there was unanimous support to bring it to all the employees."

Every new Peppercomm employee goes through the comedy training. Since word of the rather unique training has spread, it's helped Peppercomm attract young recruits who love the creative approach. But it's not a one-off deal: Employees must take refresher courses to keep the spirit of the training alive.

As Cody shared with me, "Humor has become embedded in our DNA now. The comedy training works on so many levels, in fact, it's become a rite of passage for employees which means it's turned into a huge team-building tool for us. Doing stand-up in front of your peers takes a huge amount of courage and vulnerability and it also requires a huge amount of love and support from the audience members watching their teammates perform. We see that energy transfer back to the workplace. The dynamics in our meetings are completely different once employees have done the training. Once an employee has done stand-up in front of his or her peers, doing a business presentation in front of a major client seems like a breeze!"

You've heard me say that humor isn't about telling jokes or being a stand-up comedian. Steve Cody agrees: "That's the fear most people have and we tell them unequivocally that it's not about telling jokes. It's about telling stories. We ask them to tell us a story about something that drives them crazy or something that makes them angry and then in the comedy workshops we help them make that story funny. We help them find the humor in their pain."

As a communications expert, there's a valid reason Cody champions the importance of storytelling. Stories are one of the world's oldest and most effective forms of communication because they engage and connect people. If you're trying to create a change in behavior, cold, hard facts rarely do the trick. To inspire change, you need to connect emotion with reason, link minds to hearts, fire up passions and stir imaginations. Stories are one of the most effective means of doing that. In a *Fast Company* article on the importance of storytelling, Peter Guber, CEO of LA's Mandalay Entertainment, described stories as "state-of-the-heart technology" because of their tremendous capacity to engage us emotionally.

In his book, *How to Argue and Win Every Time,* Gerry Spence recounts how it is he never lost a criminal case as either a prosecutor or a defense attorney: He never spoke like a lawyer. He spoke to juries conversationally and he told state-of-the-heart stories to help make cases more relatable and to help the jury keep track of complex arguments.

Research shows that people remember details of things much more effectively when they are embedded in a story. In fact, it's quite likely that the human brain is hardwired for stories. Chip and Dan Heath, the authors of *Made to Stick: Why Some Ideas Survive and Others Die,* believe that stories are powerful for two reasons: They provide stimulation (the knowledge to act) and inspiration (the motivation to act).[9]

Every organization has stories to tell as well: The story of its founding, of epic battles lost and won, of its colorful characters and pivotal milestones. These are stories you need to nurture and tell and retell to your customers and your employees. These are the stories that define who you are and where you're going.

On a smaller scale, any message you need to convey can be turned into a story as well. *Any* message. Suppose, for example, you want to stress the importance of your core values. You could put together a series of PowerPoint slides listing the values alongside a dictionary definition of each and then... you know... um... sorry... I nodded off just writing that sentence. Or, you could turn it into a story. You could share the experience of how Randy, only four months on the job, did something outrageously wonderful with one of your long-time customers, how Jennifer made a huge difference to the outcome of a project and how Alex's actions last week exemplify what you mean when you talk about the need for employees to demonstrate integrity in everything they do.

Incidentally, as a bonus, one study found that humor can help overcome some serious story or speech delivery flaws. In the experiment, people listened to a presentation that was purposefully disorganized, with nearly one-third of the sentences rearranged randomly. When the disorganized talk included humor throughout it, the listeners rated it far more organized than the version that included no humor.

There are entire books written on the art of storytelling, so my point here is simple: Stories are an extremely underutilized means of communicating messages in most organizations, so make use of your stories to win over hearts and minds.

As the employees at Peppercomm will gladly tell you (likely through a very funny tale), stories are also a natural conduit for humor. It's difficult for humor not to find a toehold in even the most serious of stories, so making more space for more stories also opens the door to more humor in your workplace.

## BEING OUTRAGEOUS CAN MAKE YOUR MESSAGE CONTAGIOUS

Dave Carroll's life changed the day United Airlines broke his guitar.[10] On his way to a gig with his band, *The Sons of Maxwell*, Carroll was astonished to see the baggage handlers outside his plane tossing about his prized instrument. Astonishment morphed into months of frustration and anger upon discovering the guitar was severely damaged and that the airline wouldn't pay for it because of what amounted to a policy loophole. So Carroll sought recourse the only way he knew how. He wrote a song. In fact, he wrote three songs about the saga and produced three corresponding music videos.

Like the Johnson & Johnson video, the first music video went viral on YouTube, with over a million views in four days (at the time of writing, the video has reaped over fourteen million views). The story is estimated to have touched one hundred million different people worldwide. It took Carroll two days to produce the first video, at a cost of about $150. Meanwhile, United Airlines stock dropped 10%, representing a loss of $180 million. They most definitely were *not* laughing all the way to the bank.

Yes, the song touched a nerve with disgruntled passengers and customers everywhere who salivate at the thought of meting out such sweet revenge. Yes, Carroll and his band are great musicians so they created a catchy little ditty. But what likely made the video a phenomenon was the use of humor. Lyrics such as, "I should have flown with someone else or gone by car... because United breaks guitars," and hilarious visuals sent the video soaring.

If you want people to internalize your safety messages, embody your corporate values, understand the latest changes to the policy manual or *finally* figure out that it's not cool to leave a festering stack of dishes in the lunchroom sink, don't be afraid to try something a little *déjà new* that will help your message go viral... even if the virus only needs to spread throughout the fourth floor.

It's no shocker that humor helps grab a hold of people's attention. There's a reason, after all, that US advertisers spend between $20 and $60 billion dollars a year trying to make people laugh, and why about 70% of all the Super Bowl ads use humor.[11] As ad man Arnie DiGeorge says, "In a world of clutter, you must entertain before you educate."

In an office full of emails, texts, memos, reports and endless distractions, it can't hurt to be a little entertaining to help your messages cut through the miasma. Using humor to deliver a message is akin to the sugar in the coffee syrup trick: It makes any message go down easier without ramming it down anyone's throat.

In his book, *Humor in the Advertising Business*, Fred K. Beard reviewed current research into the benefits of humor in advertising.[12] Here are some of his more telling findings:

- Humor helps attract attention;
- Humor can enhance memory and comprehension;
- Humor is, in some situations, more persuasive than neutral appeals;

- Humor tends to enhance the likability and credibility of the source;
- How much people like ads is one of the biggest predictors of sales success (likeability matters).

Of course humor doesn't always work. We've all seen ads that have attempted to use humor and flopped miserably, maybe because they're offensive or simply not funny. Or sometimes the message gets lost because the humor overpowers the message. So this all comes with a careful reading of the fine print. The point is that if humor—when done right—can help advertisers sell their wares effectively, it can help you deliver important workplace messages, too.

All of the extensive research into the use of humor in advertising agrees with one central tenet: To be effective, humor needs to be relevant. Humor for the sake of humor can certainly grab attention and make people feel good, but to be persuasive, humor needs to relate directly to the product or message. Oh and the humor needs to be funny. Go figure.

A study reported in the *Journal of General Psychology* found that humor can, under certain conditions, be highly persuasive when presenting a message that people may disagree with because the humor serves as a distraction.[13] When people know they are being sold something or know they are trying to be persuaded of something they disagree with, they tend to immediately rehearse counter-arguments. But distract them with humor and they are more likely to be persuaded.

Of course there are many variables depending on the message, the product and the audience. A study in the *Journal of Advertising*, for example, came to the rather obvious conclusion that people with a high NFH (need for humor in their lives) respond better to humorous ads than people with a low NFH.[14] (You too can sound like a humor researcher by asking people at your next dinner party what their NFH factor is.) Younger, well-educated men tend to respond best to humor. Smart people with a high NFH enjoy—wait for it—intelligent humor.

You don't need to hire a Wall Street ad firm the next time you're starting a workplace campaign to encourage people to wash their hands or fill out their tax forms correctly. But taking the time to think outside the memo or brainstorm a few creative and funny approaches with colleagues will likely pay off in the long run. Again, it's about being effective, not efficient. It's about getting results.

So when shoppers see those signs popping up in more and more stores reading, "Any Unattended Children Will be Sold to the Circus," or "Unattended Children Will Be Given a Free Espresso and a Puppy," the hope is that people will smile, perhaps like the store owner a little more and, most importantly, get the point without having to be hammered over the head.

A simple sign that evokes a smile can do wonders, but sometimes more outrageous tactics are needed to send an effective message. In 2007 the mayor of Bogota, Columbia deployed 400 mimes throughout the city to encourage pedestrians and motorists to behave responsibly. The program was a huge success. (Just when you thought it was okay to start hating mimes again.)

Regardless of how serious the message is, a bit of humor can help. The Saanich Police Department on Vancouver Island, British Columbia increased the number of visitors to their website by a third when they started using witty, attention-grabbing headlines such as, "The Stupid Criminal of the Month Award," "A Mr. Bean-Style Robbery," "The Chip Bandits," and "Who Wears a Balaclava During Summer?" Some of the press releases have even gone viral because of their humorous tone.

Going viral is, of course, everyone's dream goal when communicating in cyberspace. Advertisers, product managers, aspiring rock bands and wannabe film-producers all pray to the social media gods that their latest upload to YouTube will go viral. While humor certainly isn't the only way to hit the viral jackpot, a cursory scan of the most popular online videos in any given year shows that people clearly have a fondness for sharing videos that are outrageously funny.

In their book, *Viral Video Manifesto,* Stephen Voltz and Fritz Grobe recount how numerous businesses have laughed all the way to the bank by creating ridiculously contagious videos.[15] Blendtec's "Will it Blend?" series of quirky videos showing various objects being ripped to shreds in one of their blenders (ranging from a Justin Bieber doll to an iPhone) has been viewed by millions around the globe, boosting sales of their blenders by 700%. No matter how you slice it, those are impressive numbers.

A video featuring a dancing flash mob at a Liverpool train station has been viewed by tens of millions of people. At the end of the video a brief message appears: "Life's for Sharing—T-Mobile." What Voltz and Grobe refer to as the "light branding" by T-Mobile in this video contributed to a 22% increase in sales of T-Mobile handsets.

Before we slide too deeply into the realm of marketing and advertising (an entire book unto itself), I want to loop back to the central point. Humor can clearly help companies laugh all the way to the bank when it comes to promoting their brand and products and it's well worth your while to consider using either a little or a lot of humor in your next campaign. But the broader message in terms of creating a successful culture that drives business success is this: If using humor and daring to be a little outrageous can help you stand out in cyberspace or during the Super Bowl, then there's no reason it can't help you achieve any of your business communication goals as well.

## MEETINGS THAT INSPIRE

No discussion of effective communication in the workplace is complete until we've broached the phenomenon known the world over as "death by meeting." ("Death by PowerPoint" is a popular subset of the whole death-by-meeting experience.)

Despite the fact that it seems like half the Amazonian rainforest has suffered at the hands of countless articles and books offering ideas on how to make meetings more effective and fun, these necessities of work life continue to be a time-sucking, soul-zapping and productivity-draining source of stress for too many people.

Most organizations need to go on a meeting diet... or at least trim the length of their meetings. This is especially true in light of a U.K. study that found the average office worker spends some *sixteen hours a week* in meetings and about a quarter of that time is wasted.[16] As one of my clients once bemoaned, "I have so many meetings to attend I don't have time to go to some of my other meetings."

It's not just an issue of quantity; quality is at play here as well. After all, meetings don't kill people. People kill meetings. But it doesn't have to be that way.

As a starting point, try to set a basic goal for all your meetings: Attendees will leave feeling more inspired about things than when they arrived. Will you always achieve that goal? Maybe not, but setting it will surely help you raise the bar.

And yes, meetings should be fun! After all, what's more fun than gathering with a group of colleagues who share the same aspirations for success? What's more fun than finding out what people are working on and what milestones have been reached? What's more fun and inspiring than contributing ideas and energy toward a common cause and engaging in thoughtful conversations about the future?

If this all sounds foreign to you, the way to start making your meetings more *fun* is by making your meetings more *effective*. Make your meetings actually mean something. Make them worth coming to and worth talking about. After all, the #1 reason people don't enjoy meetings is that they view them as a waste of time.

Start with the basics. Do your team leaders have the skills to run an effective meeting? Do you always have an agenda? Do you start and end meetings on time? Do you invite only people who really need to be there? Do people understand the purpose of the meeting? Does everyone have the opportunity to be heard and participate? Are people engaging in thoughtful and respectful conversations and debates? Do you have a clear call to action at the end of your meetings and do people understand who's doing what by when? Finally, are you putting the humor advantage to work to help you achieve these goals?

For example, if you want people to read the agenda and do any pre-meeting work, make it fun! If you want people to show up on time, create a fun ritual to open up the meeting. If you want people to follow the meeting rules without beating them over the head with a copy of Robert's Rules of Order, assign a "meeting ref" to monitor the meeting with a playful touch. If you want people to avoid using jargon, create a drinking game during your meeting wherein everyone takes an exaggerated gulp of their coffee/tea/water whenever anyone uses an annoying acronym or buzzword term. Or let people know they have to sing a Celine Dion song if they arrive late to the meeting.

If you want to keep your meetings short, do what some Google teams do: Record the length of your meetings and then try to beat your best time (of course you never want to sacrifice quality for the sake of brevity, but this could be helpful for 'team huddles' or information-sharing meetings). Or try what some companies do and remove the chairs—it's amazing how quickly things will speed up and how the overall tone of the meeting changes. For something a little wackier, be like the online photo-sharing site Flickr: Everyone must drink a sixteen-ounce glass of water beforehand, with the understanding that the meeting ends whenever the first person needs to go... as in *go*.

In addition to using a bit of humor to help you achieve meeting goals, remember that your meetings reflect and help build your culture. If you want to be known as an inspiring, fun, awesome place to work, then your meetings sure as heck better be inspiring, fun and awesome as well!

By the same token, meetings are a natural place to have culture-building conversations and activities. Opening your meetings with a "values moment," where you share a story that connects to one of your core values, will help reinforce your values. Doing a team huddle on Monday morning can help inspire people for the week and keep everyone informed of what's headed their way. A Friday-afternoon team huddle reviewing the highlights of the week can help everyone end the week on a high note. Honoring someone or making space in every meeting for a "shout-out" section where team members publicly recognize someone else's efforts will help reinforce a culture of positive feedback. Fun team-building activities or ice breakers can serve as trust-building exercises that help everyone get to know each other a little better. Leaving a chair empty or having a mannequin seated at a chair to represent the customer can remind people that you need to keep the customer in mind with everything you do. Holding a humor break during longer meetings—where everyone shares the funniest thing that's happened to them since you last met—reinforces the value you place on humanity and humor in the workplace.

Because there are so many simple ways to inject some playful humor into any meeting, I've compiled a list of fun meeting icebreakers on the website at www.thehumoradvantage.com. (To access the list and other bonus resources, including "20 Ways to Grow Your Sense of Humor" and a list of links to the videos referenced in the book, enter "humor-me!" into the bonus code box.)

As many businesses understand, having fun and effective meetings where you embrace the creative formula of "Ha + Ha = AHA!" really can help you laugh all the way to the bank.

### Key Messages and Ideas

1. When it comes to building an inspiring culture, communication is everything and everything is communication. Communication is an investment; it can't be treated as a byproduct or afterthought.
2. It's not just what you say, but how you say things that matters. There's a difference between being *efficient* and being *effective*. Great communicators and inspiring organizations understand the difference.
3. Building an inspiring workplace requires an intentional effort to focus on positive communication. Humor can help keep the communication more positive.
4. Humor can be an important tool to help people share uncomfortable truths in the workplace with senior managers.
5. Speaking with a human voice helps leaders and businesses soften their image and connect with their customers and employees.
6. Stories are one of the oldest and most effective forms of communication and are natural conduits for humor.
7. Being outrageous can make any message more contagious.
8. Meetings reflect and help build workplace culture. Adding more fun to your meetings will not only make them more effective, but more creative as well.

# 6

# What a Great Idea! Why Ha + Ha = AHA!

"The essence of creativity is not some special talent, it is much more the ability to play."
– John Cleese

Churning out monster hit after monster hit, Pixar Studios has laughed all the way to the bank by making audiences laugh since 1995. From *Toy Story* to *Monsters University*, Pixar has an enviable, nearly flawless track record of critical and audience acclaim. Yet their success is not by accident. The creativity and humor expressed through their animated films is driven by a culture infused with humor, play and creativity.[1] (What did you think, they'd be a bunch of grumpy dwarves slaving away under the watch of an evil queen?)

Pixar exemplifies many of the themes we've touched upon already. For example, they do a great job at celebrating success, going so far as to give a "Production Babies" credit at the end of their movies where they list any babies born to employees during the making of a movie. Humor is one of three key traits that Pixar hires for and leaders at Pixar purposefully create a light-hearted work atmosphere that encourages the use of humor to break down power structures, build trust, strengthen social bonds and, especially, spark creativity. The playful tone set by leaders and use of humor—especially during the early stages of idea development—helps ensure that everybody's voice is heard and that all ideas are given fair treatment.

So if you want your employees to feel more animated about their ideas and create your own version of movie magic, embrace Pixar's simple-yet-effective equation for creative success, namely:

Ha + Ha = AHA!

But before we get to the power of humor to drive creativity, a few ideas on creativity's importance in the workplace.

## WHY CREATIVITY IS SUCH A GREAT IDEA

I don't want to overstate things, but without ideas you're dead. Okay, so maybe I've overstated things just a tad. But ideas truly are the currency of success. Ideas are the stepping stones to a brighter future. Ideas drive every aspect of your enterprise. Ideas help build an inspiring workplace culture *and* reflect an inspiring workplace culture.

At an individual level, surveys suggest that leaders are increasingly seeking out people with the ability to not just embrace change, but to generate ideas, think creatively and lead change.

I'm not necessarily speaking about blockbuster ideas that will rock your entire universe (although those can come in handy, especially if your company is currently working on making a better—oh, I don't know, eight-track tape or beta video recorder). As much as it'd be nice to create the Next Big Thing on a regular basis, you also need to foster an environment that champions those continuous and incremental ideas that make a difference to your employees, customers and, ultimately, your business.

Keep in mind a simple but potent thought: If the pace of change in the world outside your business exceeds the pace of change on the inside, it's just a matter of time before you'll become a Kodak moment. Or Polaroid. Or Compaq. Or TWA. Or Woolworth. (Need I go on? This is starting to hurt.)

The pursuit of ideas is also a driving motivator for many employees, who are increasingly seeking out work opportunities that will allow them more creative freedom in lieu of higher salaries. In fact, studies suggest that most people are highly intrinsically motivated to be creative and when external rewards are attached to creative projects they often dampen or extinguish the creative spirit.

Asking for ideas in your workplace is one of the simplest things leaders can do, not just to motivate employees, but to recognize them as well. Think about the messages you send every time you ask for someone's input. Asking for ideas sends the message that you value that person and that you respect their judgment, wisdom and experience. Asking involves them in the process and involvement is the quickest route to true engagement.

The final reason to intentionally embrace creativity at work is because it's fun. Part of the reason being creative is so intrinsically motivating is that it's simply fun to play with ideas. As described in the book *Inside Jokes*, "There is an undeniable similarity between the joy of humor and the joy of problem solving. When we 'get' a joke we feel a sense of discovery rather like the sense of triumph when we solve a problem."[2]

As you'll see shortly, there is, in fact, an extremely cozy relationship between humor and creativity. Both are about looking at the world through a different lens, changing perspectives and saying yes when everyone else says no. As much as a playful atmosphere begets more ideas, building an environment conducive to creativity also generates more humor.

As with everything we've discussed, it requires an intentional effort to build a creative culture. My own *Humor at Work* surveys of more than 5,000 people found that the top five places people said they had their biggest light-bulb moments were:

- In the shower;
- Driving;
- Exercising;
- In bed or asleep;
- In the washroom.

Notice anything missing? Such as, perhaps, the office? Evidently work is the place where ideas go to die! (Of course, if you really want to kill ideas you can always form a committee.) Great ideas, even those that seemingly pop into your head during your morning shower, don't just fall out of the sky. (Alas, even the fabled story of the apple falling on Sir Isaac Newton's head as a source of inspiration is likely a myth.)

If you want to get more ideas and better ideas and then implement those ideas, you need to work at it. Intentionally. This means adopting a culture-wide perspective on the topic and it all starts with your hiring practices.

Much has been written about the tendency of leaders to hire or promote employees who are just like them. Of course this makes sense—who wouldn't want to spend the day with more versions of you? The problem in doing this, however, should be obvious. Sonny and Cher were a huge hit in their day; the Sonny and Sonny Show? Not so much.

Great leaders look for people who complement their talents, employees who can shore up their weaknesses and people who offer something new to the team. If you're building a creative culture, it's paramount to hire people who might not fit the mold, who deviate from the standard issue, or who shatter old stereotypes. As the old quote goes: "If you've got two executives who think alike, one of them is redundant."

Don't be fooled into thinking that creativity is highly correlated to intelligence. Studies suggest there's little correlation between the two traits. In fact, psychologist David Parker found a positive correlation between high intelligence and a *lack* of willingness to accept new ideas.

So asking potential hires what a penguin wearing a sombrero says really isn't so crazy after all. Anything that shakes up your recruiting and hiring practices to help you find the creative thinkers, the rebels, the constructive agitators and the people who color outside the lines isn't just a good thing. In this fast-paced, global, dog-eat-dingo world where things are changing faster than most of us can keep up, it's a necessity.

## CREATIVITY CAN BE TAUGHT

Bringing already creative people on board will surely help; teaching everyone to be more creative will help even more.

Contrary to the notion that some people are lucky enough to be born creative geniuses, studies suggest that at least two-thirds of people's innovation and creativity skills are derived through learning.[3] In other words, people can be taught to be more creative and by extension, organizations can learn to be more creative. So innovative companies invest heavily in creativity training. Which doesn't always involve what you might think.

I frequently comment on how many organizations seem to operate from a rulebook established in the nineteenth century. But some nineteenth-century leaders were clearly ahead of their time. Take Daniel Burnham and John Root, the architects who created the Chicago World's Fair in 1893. They understood the importance of creating an interesting work environment to spark creative thinking and reduce stress. They installed a gym in their office, played piano for employees and even offered employees fencing lessons. (Hmm... sounds like they were the Google of the 1800s.)

What do fencing lessons have to do with designing a world's fair? More than you might think. Many organizations are realizing the benefits of offering a variety of atypical training programs and classes as a way to spark creative thinking. Pixar Studios has its very own Pixar University, where employees can take up to four hours of classes each week, not just in filmmaking, but in other arts, health-related issues, or any topic of interest to their employees. The courses help boost engagement, facilitate relationship building across different departments and, Pixar believes, nurture creativity throughout the company.

Employees at the U.K. firm ?What If! (yes, that's their name) regularly participate in activities such as exotic dance lessons, tree planting and trapeze lessons to stimulate creative connections. And we've already seen the creative benefits associated with Peppercomm's stand-up comedy training.

So as much as it might help to hire professional speakers to talk about the value creativity and innovation bring to the workplace (and they surely can), don't discount the value of bringing in a chef over lunch to teach employees how to make a soufflé that never flops. Or a professional juggler, magician, chess master, mechanic, or, yes, even a fencing trainer. (You can at least take a stab at it. What's the worst that could happen?)

## ENGINEERS REJOICE! CREATIVITY IS A PROCESS

Aaron Sorkin, the creative driving force behind TV's *The West Wing* and the movie *The Social Network*, is a big fan of showers, taking six or more every day. No, he's not a germaphobe. He hits the water for the same reason my survey found that showers are a popular idea-sparking environment. When Sorkin gets stymied by a case of writer's block he retreats to the shower, then goes back to writing until he hits another rough patch. Then it's back to the shower. Rinse, write, repeat. Rinse, write, repeat.

Several studies have confirmed that showers are, indeed, a great place for the birth of ideas.[4] There's a number of reasons why this may be so. Showers are relaxing, so you shift into autopilot mode, which means your prefrontal cortex—your brain's command and control center—essentially shuts down and your brain's default-mode network fires up, allowing you to make creative connections that the conscious part of your brain might have overlooked. Harvard researcher Dr. Shelley Carson found that highly creative people are easily distracted.[5] This is also why showers help: They distract you, allowing your brain to wander about willy-nilly.

There might even be more to it than a relaxing diversion, however. Some researchers have suggested that showers stimulate a primitive human connection to water and that happy relaxed place we find ourselves transported to in a shower releases dopamine, which is thought to be a catalyst for thinking creatively.

Time of day may also be a factor. We tend to shower in the morning or end of the day when we are often feeling a bit groggy. That fuzziness also contributes to a creative state of mind. Scientists refer to this half-awake state as hypnagogia, a time when low-adrenaline arousal allows for uninhibited free-flowing thought and increased lateral thinking. Albert Einstein, no slouch in the creative thinking department, called it "combinatorial play time."

Whatever the cause, showers seem to be great catalysts for creative thinking. But that's not my primary point. My real point is that as instantaneous and as powerful as those light-bulbs-above-the-wet-head moments feel, they are neither the start nor the end of the creative process.

Another fallacy about creativity is the notion that it's a mysterious phenomenon that arrives like a thunderbolt from on high when the angels are aligned every third full moon but only after you've poured a dollop of honey onto the tip of your nose while listening to Romanian pan flautist Zamfir. Okay, maybe that's not a *common* perspective, but I do know that many people feel creativity is a mysterious force that can't be guided, coerced, or coaxed in any way. To these people, it's a genie that comes out of the bottle only when it's damned well ready to come out of the bottle.

Fortunately, this isn't the case at all. The creative process is just that—a process that can be broken down into four broad steps, each one aided with a generous dose of humor:

1. Ask and ye shall receive;
2. Create space for ideas to thrive and multiply;
3. Discuss, debate and decide on the best ideas;
4. Do something already—turn ideas into action.

The four stages of the creative process require different forms of thinking. What's more, people have different strengths when it comes to ideas. Some of your team members might be great at coming up with ideas, but implementing them and fussing over the finer details might be completely foreign territory.

Of course, this all means that diversity isn't only the spice of life, it's the key to a more creative team and organization. If you have a group full of starry-eyed dreamers who love to think up bold initiatives, but no one to bring them back down to earth or no one to turn those ideas into action, then you'll struggle innovating. Likewise, some employees may excel at selling and championing ideas, but are lousy idea generators.

Recognizing these differences serves as a reminder that no one person should be expected to carry the creative load alone: Creativity in the workplace is a team sport that, when played properly, depends on open and honest communication, trust and—as with any team sport—copious amounts of play.

Let's have a closer look at each of the four stages, with a particular eye on how humor and play can drive more creativity and innovation in your business.

## STAGE ONE: ASK AND YE SHALL RECEIVE

All ideas begin with a question. Or a challenge. Or an opportunity (which is really still a question).

So that light-bulb moment you experience in the shower really had its genesis three minutes or seven hours or sixteen days or maybe even three months *before* your shower, when a problem or question first entered your consciousness. The light-bulb moment just happens to be when your stream of consciousness coalesced into a brilliant singular idea.

It's akin to that tip-of-the-tongue phenomenon we all experience on a regular basis. You know what I mean: You and your spouse run into an acquaintance, but you just can't recall his name. An awkwardness ensues as you desperately hope that your spouse will introduce herself so you can chime in with a hearty, "Yes, sorry! I should have introduced you...." Unfortunately your spouse doesn't play her role properly, and after your acquaintance leaves smoke pours out of your ears as you try to recall his name. All you know for certain is that it starts with the letter "B."

So your mental Rolodex cycles through every "B" name you can think of. Bob? Nope. Bill? Nope. Boswick? Definitely not. (Is that even a name?) After an agonizing fifteen minutes of torture, you leave it alone. Later that evening, while out for a relaxing, romantic dinner at your favorite Italian bistro, you shatter the silence by screaming out: "Barney!" Why? Because while you were relaxed, your subconscious went to work and managed to retrieve the file. Or perhaps you glanced over at the bar, saw a knee and the random association (bar + knee) coalesced into Barney. Or maybe a small child walked past your table holding a stuffed kangaroo which reminded you of your own child's attachment to his stuffed dinosaur which reminded you of a certain purple dinosaur named... Barney.

The point is that it helps to remember there were discrete stages to the process and evidence suggests that creative people tend to spend a disproportionate amount of time thinking about what the question or problem really is.

For good reason. How you define a question, problem or opportunity can send your mind down completely different pathways. A simple example of this is a survey reported in *Psychology Today* in which people were asked this rather odd question:

"Is it okay to smoke while you pray?"

The overwhelming majority of respondents, a whopping 90%, said, "No, that's not okay."

Then the survey asked, "Is it okay to pray while you smoke?"

This time, 90% of respondents said, "Yup, that's okay!"

I'm fairly certain those are the same questions! Yet people were moved from a 90% "no" to a 90% "yes" response just by a change in the way the question was asked.

So how you frame a problem matters. A lot. Especially when you consider how much some businesses spend to solve only a symptom of a problem rather than getting to the root cause. This is where the classic "five whys" technique can help. It's a simple process that involves asking "Why?" five different times to unpeel the layers and hopefully discover what really needs fixing.

For example:

Team members are feeling overworked and stressed.
Why are they overworked?
Because employee absenteeism is on the rise.
Why is absenteeism on the rise?
Because employee morale is so low.
Why is morale so low?
Because employees feel their concerns aren't heard.
Why do they feel that way?
Because nothing they suggest gets acted upon.
Why does nothing get acted upon?
Because the committee screening ideas isn't funneling the ideas to the appropriate managers!

Bingo! Rather than zeroing in on absenteeism-related issues that might lead nowhere, the solution lies with giving proper training to the idea committee, or disbanding it altogether and creating a new system, or improving the communication channels between the committee and managers.

Of course, with this example several assumptions were made that would need to be backed up by solid evidence. Whether you use a system like this or not, the point is that taking the time to think about the real problem can save you untold dollars, time and stress.

How broadly or narrowly you frame a question will also have a huge impact on the quality of ideas you come up with. Frame it too broadly ("How can we save the planet?") and you might end up overwhelmed by a sea of unfocussed and irrelevant ideas. Frame a question too narrowly ("How can we make a better videotape?") and you risk missing out on the fact that you're not really in the videotape business.

How you word a question can also shape the ambitiousness of your ideas. How, after all, do you catch a big fish? With a big hook, of course. So how do you nab big, bold ideas? By asking big and bold questions.

As we've seen, simply changing the order of the words or changing a single word in a question can lead people to hop aboard different trains of thought, all of which arrive at completely different stations. Asking a totally different question can lead people to forget about the train altogether and instead jump onto a supersonic jet... which is where a little humor can help.

Listening to a stand-up comedy routine from someone such as Jerry Seinfeld, it's easy to see how so much of many comedians' material is sparked by asking questions. So what's up with that? Both humor and creativity are often driven by asking unusual questions. Both, after all, are about forcing a change of perspective. Asking an oddball question ("Why is the penguin wearing a sombrero?") forces unusual connections in the brain or can lead to overlooked insights.

As recounted in *The Age of Persuasion* by Terry O'Reilly and Mike Tennant, when Honda was struggling to break into the motorcycle business in the 1970s, the company was getting nowhere by asking traditional, straightforward questions to their test drivers.[6] The drivers appeared to agree that the motorcycles were well designed and reasonably priced. But would they buy one? Nope, they'd prefer a Kawasaki.

Perplexed, they tried a different question: "If Kawasaki were a celebrity, who would it be?" The top response was Clint Eastwood. "And if Honda motorcycles were a celebrity, who would they be?" The top answer: Richie Cunningham from *Happy Days*. Voila! Asking an unusual question uncovered what was really going on. It wasn't an issue with the product itself, but the image and perception of the brand.

Finally, it's important to always ask *why*. A six-year study of 500 highly innovative people—including Twitter founder Niklas Zennstrom and Amazon's Jeff Bezos—found the most important skill for innovation was asking questions. The most important questions: "Why?" and "Why not?"[7]

Speaking of questions, what does this all mean for you and your organization? Plenty. Recognizing that questions spark curiosity, demonstrate a genuine interest in employees' perspectives, move conversations forward and drive the creative process, you need to ask *a lot* of questions—you need to change the questions you ask, and you need to foster a culture that values questioning.

Front-line employees at every level in your company need to feel as comfortable asking the CEO and top managers questions as the top managers feel asking front-line employees. Which, yet again, requires a culture built on mutual trust, respect, honesty and openness.

Even new employees need to be asked for their input and ideas. It's the simplest way to engage new employees, and because they've arrived with fresh perspectives, they often have keen insights that others closer to the issue might not see. In fact, I have a theory that new employees all stop in their tracks for a moment and think, "There must be a reason they do it this way, but for the life of me I can't figure it out. But since I'm only the new guy I'll keep it to myself." But when all your new employees keep their ideas to themselves, you're potentially missing out on some that might help you laugh all the way to the bank.

Here are a few ways to help imbue the importance of question-asking throughout your culture:

- Create a question board where employees (or customers for that matter) can post the questions that are swirling around in their heads. It doesn't matter how far out it might seem. Encourage anything and everything, since questions beget more questions. Even the oddball questions ("What if we started catering to cats instead of humans?") will not only spark ideas you might not have thought of, they'll also lighten the mood and encourage more humor.

- Create an idea board where you simply pose the open-ended question, "What if...?"

- Pose a question of the month wherein everyone is encouraged to think about a single question for an entire month. Maybe it's a call to action on how you can ensure each of your core values is being lived out loud, or an ambitious question related to a significant issue, or a provocative query designed to challenge assumptions. The point is to have every mind focus on the same challenge as they go about their lives.

- Hold regular "ask me anything" coffee meetings with the senior leadership team. No PowerPoint, no speeches... just an opportunity for employees to ask questions.

- Kick off or end your meetings with a thought-provoking question. Use a question jar to randomly select questions.

- Have everyone wear "Ask me anything!" or "Ask for my input" badges. A bit cheesy perhaps, but it serves as a constant reminder.

- Take time to think about the question. Spend time in idea-generating meetings to brainstorm and debate the best possible questions before diving into the hunt for ideas.
- Always pose this question: "What question aren't we asking?"

Question everything. Challenge assumptions. Most importantly, embrace and unleash your sense of humor to help fuel curiosity in everything you do.

## STAGE TWO: CREATE SPACE FOR IDEAS TO THRIVE AND MULTIPLY

### Setting the Mood

Although asking thoughtful and challenging questions will always play an important role throughout the creative process, the second stage is encouraging space for ideas, beginning with the physical space.

One of the many reasons people report having so many "aha moments" at places other than work is simply due to the random stimuli offered up by different environments. A study published in the journal *Cell Death and Differentiation* (now *there's* some light bedtime reading) looked into how an enriched physical environment impacts rodents' brains.[8] Sorting through the maze of details is a tad overwhelming, so allow me to cut to the chase, as it were: When raised in more interesting, multi-stimulatory environments the rodents' brains showed higher rates of synaptogenesis and more complex dendrite arbors. I don't want to overhype the importance of the rate of synaptogenesis in your office, (and don't even get me started on dendrite arbors), but perhaps this is something worth considering: Rats raised in more interesting physical environments grew more neuron connections and showed greater brain elasticity; rodents raised in sterile, cubicle-like environments lost brain cells.

While it's always a bit dangerous to make the leap from rodent to human brains, these studies should give us pause. This is especially so once you consider that studies carried out elsewhere, from prisons to hospitals, have demonstrated the powerful impact our physical environment has on our moods, stress and creativity... which is why your workplace might want to invest in its own version of the Thinkubator.™

The Thinkubator is a world-renowned creative meeting space located in the heart of downtown Chicago, featuring funky designs and furniture, bright colors, a jukebox, scent sampler, wood-burning fireplace, fun toys, video games and eighteen-foot-high ceilings to inspire blue-sky thinking. (Speaking of that creative cliché, blue-sky thinking: One study found that the higher the ceilings, the more creative its occupants. It's as though the constraints of a low ceiling impose mental constraints on our thinking, whereas our brains are more open when the sky is, literally, the limit.) Just imagine what the name alone might do to inspire you. How could you not feel more creative spending time in a "Thinkubator?"

The *Rolling Stones'* Keith Richards had the quirky habit (he had a few) of naming his guitars and assigning them a personality. He played a lot on Malcolm, for example, on their megahit *Satisfaction.* Quirky, to be sure, but also perhaps with a purpose in mind: How you label something can change how you view it... and perhaps inspire your creative muse. So if you want to infuse a bit more creative energy and fun into your workplace, renaming your meeting space is an easy way to start.

In order to not just inspire but also to help employees find their way, the meeting rooms at Google HQ are named in alphabetical order for different geographic locations. In San Francisco, their offices are named for TV shows and movies set in the San Francisco area, such as *Charmed* and *X-Men*. Their Washington office includes meeting spaces with names such as *The Situation Room* and my favorite, *The Secret, Undisclosed Location.*

YouTube's meeting rooms are named for video games, while Microsoft pays homage to its history. One Apple Computer office named its rooms after characters from *The Wizard of Oz*; Yahoo has rooms named after Ben and Jerry ice cream flavors; and MLC Corporation has a Zen Den. Some companies have named their meeting rooms to honor employees, local heroes, local attractions, or products they offer. Others have named them for their core corporate values, while still others have tied the names more closely to a creativity theme, with names such as "Inspiration Corner," "The AHA Room," and the "Room for Wow!"

Bonus points go to the Yahoo offices in Santa Clara, California, where conference rooms have names such as Coherent and Disposed, so that when someone asks where Jennifer is, the person gets to respond: "She's in Coherent."

Naming your rooms something fun is a simple way to inject some levity and to set up expectations. If you want people to be inspired during your meetings, then meeting in the "Idea Lab" sends a message.

But of course it takes more than a catchy label to inspire people. The entire design of the Thinkubator is intended to fuel the creative spirit. More and more workplaces are appreciating the impact that design has on employees and on their level of creativity. Remember, this is where many people spend the bulk of their waking hours. Shouldn't we strive to make our workplaces as comfortable, as welcoming, as homey as possible?

If the physical environment can stimulate creative thinking, shouldn't workplaces embrace a Zappos- or Google-like approach to fun, creative office space where employees are allowed to personalize, even "humorize" their environments?

Artwork, bright colors, plenty of plants and natural lighting can help, but since we're talking about laughing all the way to the bank here, funny artwork, walks of fame, crazy photo walls, wacky mascots, humor bulletin boards, fun toys and props in your meeting rooms and even dedicated humor rooms can lighten moods and serve double duty by offering up some creative stimuli.

Some companies, again most notably Pixar Studios, have intentionally designed their work environment to encourage serendipitous encounters between employees, recognizing (and confirmed by several studies) that a major source of creativity is simply the cross-pollination of ideas that result when people interact with each other.

Of course, there are other tangible factors that influence creativity. Research into the relationship between music and creativity suggests that light classical or light jazz music is most conducive to creativity.

In a paper entitled, "Is Noise Always Bad? Exploring the Effects of Ambient Noise on Creative Cognition," researchers from the University of Illinois found that a Goldilocks level of noise was just right when it comes to creativity.[9] Too much noise and the brain can't process information; too little and there's not enough abstract processing going on. But just the right amount of noise (such as the din of a moderately noisy coffee shop) helps drive creativity. Dilbert cartoonist Scott Adams, for one, prefers to work in restaurants, finding too much quiet to be quite stressful. Adams even recommends Coffitivity, an app that provides the background chatter of a coffee shop!

A research team led by Simone Ritter of the Radboud University Behavioral Science Institute in the Netherlands found the beneficial effect of sleep on creativity can be enhanced when sleepers get a whiff of orange-vanilla scent.[10] And dark chocolate, among other food items (but why even mention the others once chocolate comes up?) is thought to stimulate brain power and perhaps help fuel creativity.

The time of day or time of week can have a huge impact on creativity. Scheduling a brainstorming meeting for late Friday afternoon or first thing Monday morning when brains are overly preoccupied with other thoughts, for example, might not be the way to go. Similarly, scheduling a creative meeting for 3 pm or after a heavy lunch is probably not ideal. For best results, schedule your heavy-duty thinking assignments for mid-morning, when most brains are functioning optimally.

All these considerations—combined with a fun physical environment—can help lift spirits and, at the very least, ensure in some small measure that people don't dread coming back to work every Monday morning. But if that's all you do, it's literally just window dressing. Without a *psychologically* safe space for ideas to thrive, the funkiest creative space on the planet will go to waste.

Brazil-based Semco company has an "Out of Your Mind!" committee whose sole purpose is to meet and discuss "crazy" ideas that don't fit into the agenda of a normal meeting. The guiding principles are to present ideas based on liberty, respect for others, the power of sharing and (my favorite) the right of indolence. If other people don't respond to someone's idea with a hearty, "You're out of your mind!" the idea is considered too tame!

But a concept like this only works when the underlying culture supports it. This is why it bears repeating that creativity doesn't happen in isolation. And it sure as heck doesn't happen in an environment of closed communication, micromanagement, low morale and oppressive seriousness. Studies have shown that creativity jumps when employees have a more positive perception of their overall workplace culture. When employees see ideas being treated as a valuable commodity at work (even when their own ideas get rejected), they are more likely to contribute. A culture built on trust, open communication and plenty of humor creates the right conditions for creativity to thrive on a regular, ongoing basis.

That should be the ultimate goal. After all, the creative muse doesn't punch a time card. You can't just schedule brilliant ideas to arrive every Thursday morning during your weekly team meeting, no matter how much coffee, chocolate, and orange-vanilla scented candles you deploy. Realistically, though, you need to create dedicated times to go hunting for your creative muse, and you'll need help beyond simply setting the stage to spark some brilliant ideas.

### Storming the Brains

The concept of brainstorming has likely been around since a tribe of primitive homo sapiens passionately exchanged ideas on how best to deal with that pesky saber-toothed tiger that's been picking everyone off. The term, however, was first used by famous ad man Alex Osborn in his 1942 book, *How to Think Up*. Osborn described brainstorming as "a conference technique by which a group attempts to find a solution for a specific problem by amassing all the ideas spontaneously by its members." He proposed four simple rules for an effective storming of the brains:

- No criticism of ideas;
- Go for large quantities of ideas;
- Build on each others' ideas;
- Encourage wild and exaggerated ideas.

There's nothing overly complicated about these rules. As someone who has facilitated hundreds of brainstorming meetings I can attest to the fact that they can work quite well. The central theory is premised on two primary notions: At the early stage of the creative process, divergent thinking is the name of the game... so the more ideas the better. So yes, you'll likely generate forty-eight insanely crazy ideas that may not lead anywhere, but it's idea number forty-nine that might just be a winner, and perhaps you wouldn't have thought of idea forty-nine unless you went through the first four dozen.

The focus on quantity is important. To use a baseball metaphor, you don't hit it out of the ballpark unless you take a hell of a lot of swings. Which is why successful businesses need to keep the ideas steadily flowing. Writers for the satirical newspaper *The Onion* pitch an average of six hundred newspaper headlines a week to find the eighteen or so finalists they run with. In the book *Weird Ideas That Work,* Robert I. Sutton reveals how Skyline toys generated 4,000 ideas for new toys in one year.[11] Of those, 230 were promising enough to be worked up into a prototype, and of those only twelve ultimately became toys that sold.

The second key principle to brainstorming is something I forget whenever I walk into an Adam Sandler movie: Suspend all judgment. The theory is that you don't want to prematurely shoot down someone's potentially brilliant, bankable idea (at least until you have enough facts to do so). Prematurely killing an idea is like scrambling an egg before it's had a chance to grow into a potential golden goose. Plus, it's a very effective way of demoralizing people, since everyone truly is in love with their own idea… at least at first blush.

In fact, research supports the notion that there are practical reasons for suggesting impractical ideas. Doing so helps people generate counterintuitive ideas and forces them to question assumptions and dogma.

Some teams take the time to list their favorite idea-squashing, dream-destroying, soul-sucking phrases… all of which should be banned from any brainstorming meeting:

> "We tried that in 1964…"
> "What have you been smoking?"
> "It'll never work!"
> "We don't have the time/money/brains to pull it off."
> "If it's such a great idea, why isn't someone already doing it?"
> "But…"

At least in theory, brainstorming is one big, happy, high-energy love-fest of potentially seismic ideas, all trying to muscle their way to the top of the class. Or, it's a roomful of blank faces all looking at each other while a cricket chirps quietly in the background. (But trust me, that rarely happens.)

As much as brainstorming has been touted for decades as *the* idea-generating technique of the century, many recent studies have pooh-poohed its effectiveness. Creative types have even debated the merits of brainstorming. For example, a University of California-Berkeley study by Charlan Nemeth split 265 people into teams of five, with each given the same problem to solve.[12] Each team was then randomly assigned one of three categories: One-third of the teams were given no instructions; one-third were told to use standard brainstorming techniques with no blocking or judging being allowed; and one-third were told to brainstorm but to also criticize and debate the suggestions offered up. The results: The brainstorming groups outperformed the no-instructions group, but the debaters generated 25% more ideas than the pure brainstormers.

There seems to be a roughly fifty-fifty split: Half the studies demonstrate that brainstorming works well, while the other half say it's better to work alone or engage in vigorous debate. Based on my experience, brainstorming can work exceptionally well. This doesn't mean it's the *only* thing you should do, but it can be useful if for no other reason than to remind everyone of the need to be thinking of ideas on a regular basis and to suspend criticism before you actually know whether there's merit to an idea.

The key to effective brainstorming is to maximize the odds of it working effectively for you. Here are a few tips on how to do that.

- Meet in an interesting or unusual place, like a city park or the zoo. If all creativity requires a change of perspective, moving your meeting location can be yet another way of doing that. Conversely, convert your meeting space into a creativity zone by adding fun props, toys, reading material and inspiring graphics on the walls.

- Remind everyone of your brainstorming rules and that this is just the first stage of the creative process. This is critical because you'll always have people arriving at a meeting who were lucky enough to be born with *the* right answer to every dilemma. You need to thank those people for their great ideas, and remind them that the key to success lies in gathering as many ideas as possible... so you're going to keep looking, just in case there's something even better out there.

- Remind people that you won't make any decisions at this meeting. This is key because, as we've already seen by peeking into Aaron Sorkin's showers, ideas need time to incubate, swirl and recombine with other ideas. One study found that if you allow ideas to incubate, there's a 33% chance of making creative connections between previously unrelated ideas.[13] Plus, we've all been to meetings where twenty-four hours later we thought to ourselves, "Why didn't I speak up! I mean, seriously, Ben Affleck as Daredevil? What?" A cooling-off period is a critical way to help ensure the best idea rises to the top.

Indeed, as the book *Thinking, Fast and Slow* by Daniel Kahneman stresses, there's a need to encourage thinking at two different speeds.[14] Move quickly and you'll put forward ideas that you might otherwise hold back because your inner critic doesn't have time to interfere. Conversely, relaxed "shower thinking" can also generate creative ideas. You need both a simmer and a rapid-boil approach.

- Diversity is the spice of a good brainstorming team, since the whole point is to riff off ideas offered up from people with unique perspectives.
- If you begin to lose steam, try changing the question. As we've seen, this usually leads people down totally different paths and can reignite a good brainstorming session.
- To force a change in perspective, bring in a few clients or people from a totally different department, or an artist, entrepreneur or comedian, or even a few ten-year-olds. The Fluor Corporation in Irvine, California brought in local schoolchildren to brainstorm ideas on how to improve their workplace and found that with a mix of children and adults the group generated more ideas than the adults-only group. When brainstorming works well it's typically because you have a group of people with different backgrounds and perspectives looking at an issue through very different lenses, so what could be better than widening your field of vision?
- Have everyone anonymously submit their ideas before the meeting, then brainstorm using those ideas as a starting point... without attaching them to specific personalities. The group must only focus on the merits of the idea,

without being biased by the source. (Because as much of an idiot as Brad usually is, even he has some brilliant insights at times.)

- Break larger groups into smaller groups of two or three members. Even when the group is only five or six, there may be introverts (anywhere from 30 - 50% of the population is thought to be introverted) who are less inclined to speak up in front of the larger cohort. This helps to encourage more voices around the table.

- Try some "extreme-storming," where people brainstorm ideas by taking things to outrageous extremes and exaggerations.

- Try what Pixar Studios does. After a certain period of time has elapsed, add a twist that seemingly goes against the core tenet of brainstorming: Allow people to debate and criticize ideas, but with a "Yes and..." approach wherein people must add to and strengthen existing ideas with positive language to try and improve on them. Pixar calls it "plussing" and this technique is what turned *Finding Nemo* into the Academy Award-winning monster hit that it became and, as we'll see, is what saved *Toy Story 2* from potential disaster.

- Another technique Pixar Studios is known for is its anti-hippo approach, with hippo being a sort-of acronym for the "highest paid person in the room." In far too many organizations, brainstorming fails because participants cede to ideas offered by the most senior, loudest, or most articulate person in the room, often giving them too much credence and overlooking potentially phenomenal ideas that might originate elsewhere.

  A Harvard study by Amy Edmonson and James Detert found shockingly high levels of fear associated with employees speaking up at work.[15] In fact, even the phrase "speaking up" suggests the idea of communicating to someone of higher authority or power. So to ensure that everyone is heard equally, Pixar leaders are encouraged to set a playful tone in all meetings and to use plenty of humor to encourage everyone to speak up as equals.

Speaking of setting a playful tone, the final tip for an effective brainstorming session is to ensure there is a lot of laughter and fun, so we can't leave this discussion without a look at just why it is that Ha + Ha = AHA!

## Why Humor and Creativity are a Match Made in Inspiring Organizations

It's worth taking the time to consider why humor and creativity are such close cousins, if only to reinforce the need to intentionally build a fun workplace culture and not leave humor to chance.

Indeed the relationship is so close that some researchers even consider humor to be a subset of creativity. Others believe that although they are strongly linked, humor and creativity ought to be considered separate-but-overlapping domains. From my perspective, I go back to the rubber-chicken-and-egg cycle: It takes creativity to generate humor, and thinking humorously lays many creative eggs.

Several experiments have demonstrated that humor drives creativity. Israeli psychologist Avner Ziv found that verbal creativity test scores for tenth-grade students improved considerably after they listened to a comedian.[16]

A team of researchers found that a common characteristic of highly creative people was the high level of connectivity in their brains at rest.[17] One way to enhance that connectivity? Yup—humor.

Studies by University of Maryland psychologist Alice Isen also found that positive emotions support greater creative thinking.[18] In Isen's study, humorous films were found to create mirthful feelings in participants, which translated into enhanced creativity. Isen also found that groups who were first shown funny bloopers successfully solved creative challenges at a rate of 58%, compared with only 30% for other test groups.

Harvard researcher Moshe Bar agrees with another version of my rubber-chicken-and-egg theory, having found that 1) happier people tend to come up with more ideas; and 2) if you want to be happier, come up with more ideas![19]

There's certainly something to the notion that humor can shift us into a more positive mood. A study by Teresa Amabile and Steven Kramer found a 50% increase in the odds of having a creative idea on days when people were in a positive mood, and this creative bump can last up to two days.[2]

All of this lends credence to the craziness that some teams exhibit before or during a high-energy brainstorming session. Some teams brainstorm something completely silly to lighten the mood and fire up their brains; others might try a theater improv exercise or a spirited game of Pictionary. One of my clients blows bubbles before a brainstorm; another has been known to have a water gun fight before sitting down to meet.

As a former improv performer, I can certainly attest to the benefits of using play as a warm-up. Going into a performance without any warm-up is like heading out for a run without stretching. Consider the benefits of injecting playful humor into your meetings:

- Playing a game clears minds and helps people focus on the present. It's hard to be creative when participants are stewing about a work issue or thinking about tomorrow's big meeting.

- Playing reduces hierarchical barriers. When a team plays and laughs together, it becomes a united group of people sharing a fun experience, not bosses and employees.

- Humor is a quick way to de-stress the team, both mentally and physically. It's hard to be open and creative when people are stressed.

- As we've seen, humor can put people in a positive frame of mind where they are focused on the *possibilities*, not the *probabilities*, of things not working out.

- Humor is good for the brain! It enhances mental flexibility, helps people process incongruities better and, according to research by Dr. John Allman from Caltech, helps sharpen intuitive thinking skills.[21]

- Play encourages greater participation and communication by everyone on a team.

- Play, especially when it's in the form of a theater improv exercise, can lower people's inhibitions and create a safe

> environment for risk-taking. By lowering inhibitions, it's hoped that participants will feel far more comfortable throwing out truly wild ideas that they may have otherwise kept to themselves.

As Tina Fey outlines in *Bossypants,* the key principles of comedic improv are perfectly aligned with the goals of an energetic brainstorming session and a creative culture: Be present; always agree with an initial offer and say "Yes;" build on ideas with a "Yes and..." approach; and adopt a mindset that there are no mistakes, only opportunities.[22] Again, the research supports real-world results: In an MIT study on creativity, improvisational comedians generated an average of 20% more ideas when asked to brainstorm new product ideas, and the ideas they generated were rated 25% more creative than those of the "professionals."

I haven't seen the role of play at work better summarized than in the words Milliken, the manufacturing and design company we met earlier, uses to describe their overarching philosophy:

> "The spirit of play invigorates the curiosity to discover, the liveliness to imagine, and the will to take initiative. The openness of play encourages transparency, trust and risk-taking. The creative energy of play uncovers unique insights, stimulates deep scientific inquiry and inspires meaningful design—from these our innovations are born.... Purposeful play makes us a team. It is why our customers want us on their side. Because we play with purpose, we play with passion, we play to win."

It's no small wonder that a *Humor at Work* survey of more than 800 people found that the preferred catalysts for creative thinking are play and humor.

There's likely a tangential link to what some companies do to encourage ideas in their business. Toshiba, HP, 3M, WL Gore and Google allow employees anywhere from 10 - 20% of their work time to work on their own projects and ideas—whatever they are passionate or curious about. All of these companies have experienced tremendously innovative ideas as a result. Google's program, for example—known as Innovation Time Off—has led to the creation of about half of all their new products, including Gmail and AdSense.

Of course, once you've generated brilliant ideas, you're going to need to keep a sense of humor as you move onto the final two stages of the creative process: Deciding on the best idea, and acting on it.

## STAGE THREE: DISCUSS, DEBATE AND DECIDE

So you've got all these amazing ideas and now you need to choose one... and actually act on it. This, of course, begs the question: "Why did we come up with so many ideas in the first place?"

Now that I've said you need a lot of ideas to succeed, let's look at the down side of the equation. (Did I mention creativity is messy?) Many people and companies drown in a sea of "analysis paralysis" because they're overwhelmed with too many ideas. Yes, this does happen and there's no easy solution. But consider this: Given the alternative, it's a great problem to have!

Selecting the best idea is an entire topic unto itself. All I want to do here is to finish the creative storyline, which means embracing three ideas:

1. Nothing happens until you actually do something. AFA JCDecaux has a large yellow sign in its meeting space emblazoned with the phrase: Blah, blah, blah... ACT NOW!

2. One of the most sure-fire ways of destroying the creative energy in your workplace is to do nothing but talk about the need for creative ideas without ever acting on them. Your success will be measured by your accomplishments, not your intentions.

3. Culture is king. How successful you are at implementing your ideas will largely be influenced by the type of culture you've created.

Humor, once again, helps. As we've seen, the idea-generating stage requires divergent thinking, what some creativity experts refer to as innovative intelligence. It also requires a safe space where everyone is free to suggest any idea, no matter how outrageous it may seem at the time. In other words, the goal at the idea-generating stage is to ensure there is zero risk in bringing forward an idea. Indeed there should be zero risk, because at this stage all you're doing is talking.

But now, innovative intelligence must be trumped by analytical intelligence. Divergent thinking must shift toward convergent thinking. The risk of actually implementing a new idea must be carefully weighed. This is where things get messy and why there's no silver bullet to all this.

At the stage of cheerily announcing "there's no such thing as a bad idea," it's useful to share all the examples of ideas that were famously pooh-poohed but turned out to be brilliant ideas:

- High speed rail travel is impossible because people will suffocate—Unknown;
- What can be more palpably absurd than the prospect held out of locomotives traveling twice as fast as stagecoaches? *The Quarterly Review*, March, 1825;
- Who the hell wants to hear actors talk?—Harry Warner, Warner Brothers Studios;
- What use could this company make of an electrical toy?—William Orten, president of Western Union, speaking to Alexander Graham Bell about his new-found invention, the telephone;
- There is no reason for any individual to have a computer in his home Ken Olson, president, chairman and founder of Digital Equipment Corporation.

There are thousands of idea-squashing quotes that remind us not to prematurely shoot down the seed of an idea that may one day bloom into an amazing success story.

But here's the rub. One can also generate a list of insanely stupid ideas that never should have seen the light of day. Ideas that wasted countless dollars, time and energy:

- New Coke;
- The Edsel;
- Celery-flavored Jello (yes, they actually tried this);
- The McLobster.

Need I go on? We could easily brainstorm a list of thousands of failed companies, products, TV shows, movies and hairstyles (yes, I got a perm in ninth grade and no, I don't remember why I thought that would be a good idea).

Picking winners from losers is easy in hindsight, but when you're in the throes of debate, it's never easy. It requires a balancing act. If everyone on your team opts for one big cuddly love-in, peer pressure might encourage people to "go along to get along", resulting in dangerous ideas being adopted or the best idea being overlooked in favor of consensus. If your culture is too risk-adverse you're in danger of always choosing the safest route; too trigger-happy and you might overlook some serious risks. There's no question that finding the best idea is often a balancing act, which, come to think of it, may not even be the right term when you consider that the best ideas are often along the margins and not in the mushy middle ground associated with compromise.

Here are six things you can do to improve the odds of the best idea seeing the light of day:

1. Acknowledge the inherent danger of "groupthink" (history is littered with cautionary groupthink tales and studies that demonstrate how people in a group can be easily swayed to conform to sometimes outrageous decisions). Encourage ground rules that promote honest and healthy debate focused on ideas, not on the personalities behind them.

2. As with brainstorming, split larger groups into smaller subgroups of two or three individuals to encourage greater participation, with honest opinions being shared.

3. Assign a cooling-off period before making any final decisions, so people have time to let things percolate.

4. Bring in an outsider (or two or three) to offer a more unbiased, baggage-free opinion.

5. Assign the role of a court jester or contrarian to challenge assumptions and provoke discussion.

6. Keep things light! Humor not only helps spark the creative process but will keep emotions in check and defuse tensions when the conversation heats up, which, if you're on the right track, it most certainly will.

There are numerous analytical rating systems and decision-making matrices that can be useful.

Some companies create prototypes or test pilot programs. Some have created spoofs of the reality TV show *The Dragon's Den* (the Canadian version) or *Shark Tank* (American version) wherein employees pitch their ideas before a team of sharks/dragons who will then challenge the pitchers with tough questions before deciding if the idea should be explored. Other companies, most notably Google, have systems whereby employees put ideas online and allow other employees to vote on their worthiness. You can try a simple pros and cons list, or do a risk analysis aiming to minimize the probability of failure and associated consequences. But in the end, true innovation requires a culture based on trust, humor and honest dialogue.

Even at our poster child for creativity, Pixar Studios, it's far from a fun-fest full of puppies and rainbows and talking toys. Kids' movies, after all, are serious business. When *Toy Story 2* was first screened internally, things got very serious… fast. Because by all accounts, the movie wasn't working. Why? Its creative team had been working in isolation without the benefit of their extensive "plussing" process. Even after everyone plussed their critical asses off, it was clear the movie was in dire straits. So with less than a year to go, the majority of the movie was trashed.

But after much stress, turmoil and heated debate, *Toy Story 2* went on to earn immense critical acclaim and box-office success and now ranks as one of the best animated movies of all time. That success would not have happened without a culture that supported open communication and trust.

## STAGE FOUR: DO SOMETHING ALREADY—TURN IDEAS INTO ACTION

None of us will ever know if an idea is truly great until we try it out. Here are three simple philosophies that many innovative companies use to guide their approach:

1. They do things to find out what they need to do next; they take a step to discover where the next step should be placed, if at all. They embrace, at least at times, the counterintuitive notion of "leap before you look".

According to Peter Sims, author of *Little Bets—How Breakthrough Ideas Emerge from Small Discoveries*, this is exactly what highly creative people and highly innovative companies often do—leap, then look.[23] In other words, as Sims says, they "do things in order to discover what to do." They share prototypes of products early on with customers to see what direction they should head in; they start projects without knowing where the finish line is; they dive into something before they have a perfect plan in place. Because just like the storyline in an animated movie plot, things will change as soon as your idea comes crashing into reality.

2. They fail fast. Again, this is a key philosophy of Pixar Studios. If people are going to be honest about mistakes, you need to change course quickly.

One of the great advantages small companies have over their behemoth rivals is the ability to change on a dime, if needed. And a failed idea is often when the true nature of an organization's culture is revealed. After all, every organization says they value creativity and innovation... until a new idea fails. That's when the knives often come out, accompanied by a hearty, cynical round of "I told you so." In some cases the offending employees may be publicly berated, given a poor review on their performance appraisal, demoted, or even fired.

When those same employees are asked a year later for their great ideas, just how far out on a limb do you think any of them will ever venture again? Conversely, organizations with a healthy culture view failure as a learning opportunity. As education. As experimentation. In truly innovative organizations, smart failure is even rewarded because they want to encourage the continual sharing of new ideas—and throwing someone under the boardroom table tends to dampen the whole creative spirit thing.

Intuit software company and Eli Lilly pharmaceuticals have held "failure parties" to celebrate what they've learned from a failure and help employees regroup after a setback. Intuit has also used the aptly named "Swing for the Fence Award" to reward employees for their smart failures. P & G encourages employees to talk about their failures during performance reviews in a positive light. Centiro Solutions, a Swedish software company, created an informal "failure club" where employees hold humorous meetings to discuss the mistakes they've made and what they've learned. But my favorite example is from the Grey Group advertising agency in New York, the same creative geniuses that came up with those hilarious talking baby e-trade commercials.

Because the company was growing so fast, there was concern it would lose its creative edge. So to encourage an ongoing spirit of risk-taking, the head of the agency instituted the Heroic Failure Award, a Stanley Cup-sized trophy that honored whoever tried an outrageously heroic idea that flopped.

The first winner of the Heroic Failure Award went to the person who suggested they collect some actual cat poop and place it under the meeting table during a pitch meeting to demonstrate to their kitty litter client how well their product worked and how passionate they were about the product. A heroic and risky idea indeed, which resulted in some shocked reactions, but fortunately, also some hearty guffaws.

3. They celebrate small wins. As we saw in Chapter Four, seeing progress at work, having a sense of momentum and celebrating small wins is one of the most important ingredients when it comes to motivating employees. Making changes in any workplace or turning any idea into a reality can be a daunting task, which is why it is critical to celebrate your small wins, champion your ideas and build momentum daily so that employees see the change happening before them.

There is nothing more motivating than when employee sees their ideas turned into action. *Nothing.*

Okay, so if you re-read Chapter Four, you'll find there are other things that are powerfully motivating as well. Which means we've come full circle, to some extent, because if your creative ideas have any hope of coming to fruition (and you better hope they do, because your business depends on it), you need to zoom out to a cultural lens and tap into as many motivational triggers as possible. You need to connect the idea to a larger sense of purpose, passionately sell it, show that progress is being made, sell the "what's in it for me?" aspect of it to make it personal, tap into people's sources of pride and, above all else, encourage people to have fun and play.

Because as much as you need a sense of humor to help spark a new idea, you'll need to double down on your humor to help sell that idea, overcome the many obstacles and landmines that lay in the idea's path, recharge your batteries and manage your stress in the face of any and all resistance.

This brings us to the next chapter: If Ha + Ha = AHA, is it possible that Ha + Ha can lower your AAAAAAH!!?

### Key Messages and Ideas

1. Ideas are the currency of success; allowing employees the freedom to be creative is highly motivating.
2. You need to be intentional about creativity at work and take a culture-wide approach. Creativity doesn't happen by accident.
3. Inspiring, innovative organizations hire and train with and for creativity. Yes, creativity can be taught.
4. Creativity is a process. Different stages require different skills and different modes of thinking.
5. Questions drive the creative process. Creative people and organizations spend a disproportionate amount of time thinking about what the real question is and asking a lot of questions.
6. Creating a physical space for creativity is important; creating a safe psychological space for creativity is essential.
7. Brainstorming with a "yes and..." or "plussing" approach can be useful in generating more ideas in a group environment.
8. Humor and play drive the creative process. They feed off each other and humor helps force a change of perspective.
9. Selecting the best idea requires a culture built upon respect, trust and open/honest communication.
10. Innovative organizations do to find out what needs doing, fail fast and celebrate small victories when new ideas are adopted.

7

# Putting Humor to Work for Less Stress and More Success

> "Laughing at our mistakes can lengthen our own life. Laughing at someone else's can shorten it."
>
> Cullen Hightower

The CIA knows something about, well, pretty much everything, I imagine. They may be monitoring our brainwaves right now for all I know. But as it turns out, they also know a bit about the effective deployment of humor, as I learned after I managed to uncover a secret CIA handbook that was discretely passed along to me in a brown paper bag by the young woman working behind the counter of my local bookstore. Turns out they're not all that secretive when it comes to humor.

Ed Mickolus's book, *The Secret Book of CIA Humor*, suggests that there is plenty of humor to be found deep within the recesses of the Central Intelligence Agency, which, given the serious nature of its work, is an intelligent thing for an intelligence agency to do.[1] (Just to clarify for the more cynical reader, I am referring to *intentional* humor deployed by the CIA, not accidental humor.)

Some of the humor is, of course, classified and if I shared it with you I'd have to track you down... and we all know how that would end. Fortunately, plenty of CIA humor isn't classified. Mickolus, a former CIA employee, was a notorious workplace prankster. In fact, so notorious that his boss laid down three rules of prankster engagement:

1. Don't be cruel;
2. Don't do anything I have to hear about;
3. Don't destroy government equipment.

Fantastic advice for any workplace hoping to minimize stress through the use of humor—and very important given that one of the central reasons to embrace humor is to reduce stress, not enhance it. Fortunately, a lot of the humor Mickolus recounts was intended to blow off steam and defuse potentially explosive situations (figuratively speaking). In fact, one of their primary mantras was something I recommend as an effective stress re-framing technique: "It could have been worse."

And there definitely are worse ways to deal with stress than by mobilizing your undercover humor resources. For instance, too many organizations simply ignore the outrageous cost of workplace stress, hope for the best... and keep buying new photocopiers every year.

## THE COST OF STRESS IS STRESSING ME OUT

An Ipsos survey found that 51% of Albertans admitted to physically assaulting a photocopier. Albertans lead otherwise-calm Canada in a strange subcategory of workplace stress, "copy rage." Of course, it's not just photocopy machines that pay the price. According to the World Health Organization, stress costs American businesses an estimated $300 billion every year.[2] The Centers for Disease Control and Prevention's National Institute for Occupational Safety and Health reports that:

- 40% of job turnover is due to job stress;
- 60% - 80% of all on-the-job accidents are stress related;
- Health care costs are 50% greater for employees with high stress levels.[3]

The Canadian consulting firm Chrysalis cites stress as the cause of 19% of absenteeism, 40% of employee turnover, 30% of disability costs and 60% of all workplace accidents.[4] In a Careerbuilder.com survey, nearly four in ten employees said one of the main attributes they'd look for in a new employer is a less-stressful work environment.[10]

Clearly, replacing photocopiers is the least of your worries.

Then there's the hidden costs of stress: Increased mistakes and conflicts, reduced creativity, the negative impacts on customer service and the increase in absenteeism's rarely discussed alter-ego: "presenteeism"—the phenomenon of employees not working at their full potential due to illness or stress. A study reported in the *Journal of Organizational Behavior* found that presenteeism is a bigger and more costly problem than absenteeism.[6]

It's not just about those employees who are obviously suffering from stress. We've all worked with people who quit many years ago, but keep showing up to collect a paycheck. Presenteesim includes otherwise hard-working employees who aren't fully engaged because they feel as though they are working in a culture that doesn't support, appreciate, or respect their efforts. Researcher Lakshmi Ramarajan found that the top causes of burnout and disengagement are a lack of respect, ideas not being valued, lack of control and the absence of any feedback.[7] Employees who felt valued and respected, on the other hand, could handle much higher levels of work without burning out or having frighteningly bad hair days.

At an individual level, stress has been linked to just about every known affliction humankind can be afflicted with, including increased rates of heart disease, diabetes and obesity. Quite simply, stress kills. Toxic work environments should be declared hazardous waste sites, because they are just as dangerous to your health.

Some companies get it, like SAS, a business analytics company I had the pleasure of visiting in Cary, North Carolina. SAS is known as one of the best places to work in the US, and strolling around its sprawling university-like campus, it's easy to see why. Home to more than 5,000 employees (and did it ever feel like a home), the campus includes on-site childcare, an on-site health care center (with a fifty-plus staff complement), deluxe fitness center and swimming pool. The company offers numerous aerobic, swimming and athletic classes and intramural leagues in a variety of sports. SAS invests heavily in employee wellness because it values employees as real human beings and encourages a healthy work-life balance.

Although many businesses are jumping enthusiastically aboard the health-and-wellness bandwagon, too many are using stopgap measures that only treat the symptoms and not the source. Companies spend, on average, eighty times more on treating symptoms rather than on prevention. In fact, it's estimated that less than 5% of the money Americans spend on health care goes toward prevention rather than cure, so putting the cart before the sick horse is a societal problem.

Fortunately, it doesn't have to be this way. Every idea in this book will reduce the stress temperature in your workplace. Every time you hold a fun event or take part in a wacky tradition or celebrate your success, you're not just building a stronger team or improving communication, you're also helping stem the tide of stress. A culture that connects employees to an inspiring sense of purpose, that models values such as trust, respect and appreciation, that recognizes and celebrates success, that communicates in an open and honest manner, and that allows employees creative freedom will naturally have lower levels of stress.

A study from the University of Michigan's Ross School of Business found that employees who "thrive" (being fully engaged in helping to create a company's future) are more productive and experience a whopping 125% less burnout than their peers.[8]

It's not just the psychological environment that matters. A study by Dr. David Lewis of 800 Hewlett-Packard employees found that half of the group assigned to work in a bright, open environment had lower blood pressure levels and 50% lower stress levels than the half who worked in a cluttered, disorganized environment.

The causes of workplace stress are as plentiful as the solutions, so extolling laughter as the best medicine in the fight against stress will only be effective if it's taken alongside a reality checkup:

- Four hours of sleep doesn't cut it, no matter how much coffee you drink;
- Eating potato chips and donuts for breakfast is *not* the breakfast of champions;
- Lifting your beer mug up and down isn't enough exercise;
- Multi-tasking just means you're doing several things poorly and making yourself more stressed out in the process;
- You can't do more with less—you really ought to start doing less with less.

So obviously humor isn't a magic elixir, but embracing a healthy sense of humor at work is still an incredibly potent antidote in the fight against stress.

## BUT SERIOUSLY, IS LAUGHTER THE BEST MEDICINE?

A rather quirky study found that dogs at an animal shelter in Spokane, Washington were more relaxed and playful when grunting noises of playing dogs were broadcast to them over the speakers.[9] The grunt-like sounds of the playing dogs sounded somewhat like laughter and seemed to have the same calming effect that laughter has on humans. So, if "dog laughter" soothes the savage beast at an animal shelter, what about us? Can a little levity lighten the load enough to make a difference?

We've heard it thousands of times: "Laughter is the best medicine." But is it really better than a good dose of penicillin or a couple of aspirin? The polio vaccine? If I get crushed by a filing cabinet should I just start laughing?

Okay, so maybe laughter isn't the *best* medicine. But we all know it makes us feel better, because we've all experienced the good feeling that comes with an epic belly laugh. When, after all, was the last time you called an ambulance after a side-splitting bout of the guffaws?

Much has been written about the medicinal benefits of laughter. Although much of it is overhyped, there are numerous studies suggesting laughter and humor can help soothe the savage beast of stress.

Pioneering humor researcher Dr. William Fry found it takes only one minute of hearty laughter to achieve the same heart rate and potential workout benefits as ten minutes on a rowing machine.[10] So feel free to go to your local gym and laugh at the people working out.

Dr. Lee Berk found that merely anticipating laughter reduces potentially detrimental stress hormones, while laughter itself triggers gamma waves, the same brainwaves associated with meditation.[11] Other studies have found that laughter *may* lower blood pressure (once the laughing has subsided), increase the flow of oxygen to the brain (highly recommended at work), increase salivary immunoglobulin A (an antibody that fights upper respiratory infections) and improve our tolerance for pain.[12] The University of Maryland School of Medicine found that laughter increased blood flow by 22%, whereas mental stress decreased it by 35%, prompting lead researcher Michael Miller to suggest that fifteen minutes of laughter a day is likely very good for the vascular system.[13]

Researcher Michelle Newman had subjects watch a highly stressful film featuring industrial accidents narrated by people using either a serious or humorous style.[14] Three stress measures were recorded: Heart rate, skin temperature and skin conductance. The group that watched the humorous narration experienced the lowest tension and the least negative effect.

Although the studies go on and on, the science on this topic is still in its infancy. Part of what makes it challenging is separating out the benefits of laughter from those accrued by being in a more mirthful state of mind as a result of humor. But given that laughter (and I'm speaking here of positive laughter incidentally, not mad scientist laughter that guffaws at the thought of annihilating the planet) is a highly social phenomena that can unite teams—and that unto itself is a stress-reducing benefit—then it would seem the more laughter, the better.

Several humor researchers believe smiling and laughing evolved as a means of communicating the message, "I am showing you my teeth to demonstrate that I mean you no harm. See, I don't bite!" As such, more laughter at work not only reflects a positive environment, it also contributes to a more supportive atmosphere.

Even just smiling may change our physiology and help us relax. One study found that people rate the funniness of cartoons higher when they are forced to smile by holding a pen in their mouth, suggesting there may be a positive feedback loop and something to the adage "fake it until you make it."[15]

Beyond the physical benefits, humor clearly has an impact on stress because of the emotional and cognitive shifts it creates: Humor can change the way you *feel* and the way you *think*. A study that scanned subjects with an MRI while they read funny cartoons or watched clips of the British television show *Mr. Bean,* has enabled scientists to see how the brain reacts when someone gets to a punch line.[16] The parts of the brain that light up include the ventral tegmental area, the nucleus accumbens and the amygdala. (Which, if you're like me, are probably the results you expected.) These areas of the brain represent the key regions in the dopamine reward circuit. So essentially we humans all enjoy a slight high, a tiny jolt of "happy juice" every time we experience some positive humor.

A study by C.C. Moran found that exposure to just a four-minute humorous film can lead to a significant reduction in anxiety.[17] Another study contrasted the benefits of a twenty-minute treadmill run with twenty minutes of watching comedy, concluding that the comedy video produces similar results as physical exercise when it comes to boosting positive emotions and reducing emotional distress—and it led to even more anxiety-reduction than physical exercise. A study of public speakers found that watching Jerry Seinfeld or other comedians before going on to speak reduced speakers' heart rates significantly.[18] Other studies have linked humor and feelings of mirthfulness to increased levels of hope, higher levels of energy, improved perceptions of boring tasks, and enhanced enjoyment of positive events.

The benefits of humor speak to the very essence of what we mean by a "sense of humor." Like our other senses, humor can be a way of positively interpreting the environment around us. Although it won't make your problems magically disappear, humor will help you gain some much-needed perspective during a stressful event.

Humor also helps you control your reaction to stressful events. A major cause of stress is a sense of powerlessness, so tapping into your humor is a means of gaining control over your emotional reaction, a way of reminding yourself that although you can't control the universe around you, you can control how you respond to whatever the universe lobs your way. Humor also provides a welcome distraction during stressful times, and that alone is worth its weight in gold. Or at least chuckles.

A study looking at the use of humor as a coping tool by female executives found that certain styles of humor (more on that shortly) helped regulate their emotional reactions to stress, helped them take a more philosophical approach to their problems, reduced tension and helped them accept things as they were.[19]

Not to compare your office to a North Korean prison camp, but one study examined the psychological health of eighty-two surviving crew members of the *USS Pueblo* after they were released from eleven months of imprisonment in North Korea.[20] Humor was found to be one of the coping strategies of the former prisoners that was significantly correlated with better psychological health. Similarly, US military cadets that used a coping style of humor were more likely to stay in the army than those whose humor went AWOL.

Of course, there's a myriad other relationships at work. Since we tend to gravitate more toward people with a healthy sense of humor and since positive relationships are also key in reducing stress levels, humor might play a tangential role in reducing stress, simply by helping us maintain a good social network.

## ALL HUMOR IS NOT CREATED EQUAL

A study led by Adam Miklosi found that, yet again, dogs can teach us a little something about the effectiveness of humor as a stress-buster.[21] The study measured levels of the stress hormone cortisol before and after the dogs played, examining two different groups of working dogs: German shepherds who worked for the Hungarian police and German shepherds who worked at Hungarian border crossings. The results, surprisingly, were quite different. The policemen's dogs' stress levels rose, whereas the border-crossing dogs' cortisol levels decreased. Why?

It turns out the dogs, like many of us, were working in two very different cultures with two different styles of play. Whereas the police commanded their dogs to play, the border guards engaged their dogs in voluntary play.

As it turns out, bus drivers have a similar response to German shepherds. A study published in the *Academy of Management Journal* tracked a group of bus drivers for two weeks.[22] The researchers found that on days when the drivers forced a smile, their moods deteriorated and they withdrew from work. Trying to suppress negative thoughts seems to make those thoughts even more persistent. But on days when the drivers displayed more genuine smiles based on deeper efforts such as focusing on pleasant memories, their overall moods and productivity increased. It would appear, therefore, that a "fake it 'til you make it" approach only goes so far.

Finally, studies in hospitals have shown that when patients are given control over which comedy they watch on TV, the health benefits and stress-reducing results are far more positive than if they're forced to watch an Adam Sandler flick.[23] (Unless you enjoy Adam Sandler movies, in which case medical science may want to examine your brain for other reasons.)

Play, by its very nature, should be a voluntary undertaking. Recall the rubber-chicken-and-egg relationship between humor and culture: As important as it can be to intentionally use humor to build a less-stressful culture, it's even more critical to build a thriving culture wherein humor is the egg that keeps getting laid. In other words, create the conditions for positive humor to happen naturally. A simple but key principle when it comes to creating fun events at work is to give everyone an equal opportunity to participate in the fun event, but *don't force everyone to do so.*

The other lesson is that for humor to work most effectively at an individual level, it needs to be humor that works *for you*. Everyone has their own unique sense of humor, likely as unique as our finger-prints. So it doesn't matter that no one else in your office finds *Mr. Bean* funny. If *Mr. Bean* massages your funny bone better than anyone else, that's what the humor doctor would order.

Voluntary participation is important, but what matters even more on a day-to-day basis at work is the *style* of humor used, since this will largely determine its stress-busting effectiveness.

Dr. Rod A. Martin of the University of Waterloo has studied the effectiveness of different types of humor when it comes to fighting stress.[24] The Humor Styles Questionnaire helps distinguish potentially beneficial from harmful humor. The four styles defined by the questionnaire are:

- **Affiliative humor**—The tendency to tell jokes, make humorous observations and say funny things as a way to amuse others, reduce interpersonal tensions and facilitate relationships;
- **Self-enhancing humor**—Maintaining a humorous outlook even when alone, being amused by the incongruities and absurdities in life, keeping one's humor in the face of stress and adversity and using humor to cope with challenges;
- **Aggressive humor**—The tendency to use humor to criticize or manipulate other people, including sarcasm, ridicule, teasing and disparaging humor;
- **Self-defeating humor**—The tendency to amuse others by saying funny things at your own expense, to use excessively self-disparaging humor and to use humor to ingratiate yourself with others. This type of humor can also be used to avoid dealing with problems or issues in the workplace.

Though most of us shift between humor styles depending on mood and context, we tend to have a predominate style that we practice most of the time, a style that likely impacts how psychologically healthy we are. Affiliative and self-enhancing humor are, as you might guess, considered much healthier forms and have been positively correlated with lower levels of depression and anxiety and higher levels of self-esteem and overall psychological health. Aggressive and self-defeating humor are associated with higher levels of hostility, aggression and anxiety. (Which makes sense, given that the term "sarcasm" comes from the Greek "sarkasmos," which means to tear at flesh like a dog.)

The research suggests that self-enhancing is the best style when it comes to combating stress. People who score high on self-enhancing humor are less likely to stew and rehash negative past events and are healthier emotionally. In other words, your workplace needs more Jerry Seinfelds and fewer Don Rickles.

## PRACTICE SAFE WORKPLACE HUMOR

Speaking of Don Rickles (for younger readers, think Andrew Dice Clay, Gilbert Gottfried or Dane Cook), everything we've discussed so far has been predicated on the notion that you are practicing *safe* humor. By safe humor, I mean humor that laughs *with* people, not at them; humor that defuses tension and doesn't ramp it up; humor that tears down walls rather than builds barriers; humor that unites rather than divides; humor that spurs the creative process, rather than sarcastically cutting down ideas. Perhaps above all else, safe humor is humor that won't get you fired! In other words, a self-enhancing, affiliative approach, rather than an aggressive or self-defeating style of humor.

Which isn't to say—as we saw in Chapter Five—that we can't benefit from some of the more sarcastic or aggressive humor that may occasionally pop up in the workplace. Cartoonist Scott Adams has observed that the worse the economy does, the more popular his Dilbert cartoons become. Yes, employees seek solace in the cartoons, but they also might be sending a subversive message about their own work environment. Reading between the punch lines can help us understand people's true feelings about a subject.

So we need to be careful not to paint all seemingly negative types of humor as completely harmful. Black (or "gallows") humor can help people in stressful occupations maintain a healthy perspective. Emergency-room doctors, for example, sometimes share what, to an outsider, might seem incredibly inappropriate humor. But as long as they're only sharing that humor among themselves at an appropriate time and place, it might be the only thing that keeps them sane.

Having interviewed dozens of funeral home directors, I can tell you that they are highly dedicated, caring professionals who also often have a wicked sense of humor that helps them maintain that professionalism day in and day out. Remember—there's a world of difference between laughing *at* a tragedy and using humor to cope *with* tragedy.

In fact, research by Rod Martin and Herbert Lefcourt has demonstrated that people with handicaps who exhibited the highest levels of vitality and viewed their disabilities in the healthiest manner were also the most likely to laugh at cartoons that featured disabled people... which some people might find offensive.[25] (One cartoon, for example, showed a gallows with a set of stairs on one side, a wheelchair sign and ramp on the other side.) They also found that widows and widowers who were able to find humor in the face of their loss were happier and better equipped to deal with stress.

A Stanford University study found that telling jokes about terrifying or tragic events helped people cope more effectively with stress than when they acted solemnly.[26] They also found that when people used humor to reframe stressful events in funny ways, it increased their creativity, verbal fluency and cognitive flexibility.

So letting employees decompress with humor, even when it's not always 100% feel-good humor, can be important. But inspiring workplaces should always aim to foster a positive working environment where people predominantly use a healthy style of humor. To help remind employees of this, one of my clients has a "sarcasm jar" to raise money for charity. Employees must toss in a dollar every time they make a sarcastic remark.

Some workplaces even create a code of humor conduct to remind staff to keep their humor positive and that the workplace is not the place for sexist, racist, political, ethnic, or put-down humor.

Some of you might be thinking, "What's left to laugh about?" But when we consider the broader definition of humor, we remember there's a whole world of safe material waiting for us without having to dive into the gutter.

This is especially important advice for leaders. Subversive humor is a tool that allows people to regain hope and control in a seemingly powerless situation. The controversial and pioneering comedian Lenny Bruce, famous in the 1960s for his edgy and subversive humor, believed in the power of humor to give the underdog a voice and to skewer pomposity and arrogance. Charlie Chaplin's film *The Great Dictator* made Hitler a little less menacing. Subversive humor is always about the underdog leveling the playing field. So when leaders use humor that targets front-line employees, there is no upside and a whole lot of downside!

For leaders to inspire and build strong teams, their humor must stay firmly in the self-enhancing and affiliative modes, which at times means turning the punch line on themselves. In fact, one of the most effective stress-busting things a leader can do is create an event where the employees have the chance to have a bit of a laugh *at the boss's expense.*

One last thought before leaving the safe-humor talk. Some of my more conservative clients still live in abject fear that if they welcome humor into their workplace, offensive humor will suddenly spring up everywhere and anywhere. But when I ask leaders at companies such as Zappos or Beryl this question, they look at me with blank faces. It simply isn't a problem in any of the inspiring, humor-filled organizations I've researched around the globe. I suspect it isn't a problem because inspiring organizations understand that you get the kind of humor that your culture reflects. If you have a positive, supportive and respectful culture, the humor will tend toward the positive, supportive and respectful.

## THREE Rs OF EFFECTIVE STRESS-BUSTING HUMOR

There is literally no limit to how you can tap into your sense of humor to manage stress at an individual, team, or even organizational level. Most of the humor will, ideally, happen spontaneously in the moment, without any coaxing or planning. It's important to create a culture that encourages people to be comfortable enough to allow spontaneous, natural humor to come out and play whenever and wherever it's needed. However, it can also help to proactively inject some stress-reducing humor into the mix, and to have some simple strategies for tapping into your humor resources when they are most needed. Remembering these three simple Rs can help.

### Reframe

There are two key principles that can help us cope with stress, if we intentionally embrace them.

The first is that stress is in the eye of the beholder. It's not what happens to us that causes stress, it's our *interpretation* of stressful events that causes bad hair days. It's what our inner voice (or voices—I think I have a committee of twelve) is saying that has the power to turn minor events into full-blown catastrophes.

The second principle is that no matter what happens in life, we have 100% control over how we react. Easier said than done, I know. When work is overwhelming us or we feel like we're at the end of our rope with an uncooperative colleague or photocopier, it's easy for the reptilian part of our brain to take control, leading us down the path toward unrestrained photocopier violence.

Fortunately, humor can help. In fact, the ability of humor to reframe situations strikes at the heart of what having a sense of humor is all about: How we interpret the world around us. Humor doesn't make our problems disappear, but it gives us a healthier perspective by distancing ourselves from the stressful event. Let's be clear—I'm not talking about ignoring conflict at work (as a self-defeating style of humor is prone to do) because ignoring issues only creates more conflict in the long run. But humor reminds us that we have the power to choose our reaction to anything, even when we fall off the stage.

It was, naturally, while speaking at a safety conference that I chose to fall off the stage for the first (and hopefully last) time in my speaking career. Actually I really didn't choose to fall, but I did choose my reaction. I could have chosen to be embarrassed, but instead I simply rolled onto my back on the floor in front of the stage, leaned into my lapel microphone and said, "I'll now be taking questions from the floor."

Humorous re-framing can help with more than just minor slip-ups, though. When a fire broke out at Barney's Motel, then-owner

Barry Williams changed the highway sign to read: "Great Deals on Non-Smoking Rooms." Of course this was still an extremely difficult day for Williams, but re-framing the event with a bit of silly humor helped him get through.

Even the seemingly trite motto of the CIA, "It could have been worse," can provide some much-needed perspective, especially if you humorously exaggerate how the situation could have ended. Therapists use a version of this re-framing technique called "paradoxical therapy," where in certain situations and with certain patients, they will not only agree with the person's negative outlook on a situation, they'll actually explain how it's likely even worse than what the patient imagines. Offering this perspective helps the person see that perhaps they are overreacting.

The power of the inner voice shows up in research suggesting that many silver medalist Olympians are less happy with their medal than bronze medalists. Why? It's all about the inner voice. The silver medalists are focused on what could have gone better: "I lost gold. I missed it by *that* much." The bronze medalists are focused on what could have been worse, namely fourth place and off the podium altogether.

According to psychologist Martin Seligman, author of *Learned Optimism*, it's possible to re-train our brains to help us focus more positively and optimistically.[27] Seligman suggests that naturally pessimistic types tend to view stressful events in three ways: They take it personally, they think it'll affect every aspect of their life, and they think that the impact will last forever. But his research has shown that people can re-train their inner voice, so that when negative events happen they can essentially come to the healthier perspective: It's not personal, it's not going to ruin their entire life, and it's only a temporary setback.

Having a simple mantra such as "It could have been worse," or "I really didn't order this today," or "Beam me up Scotty," or "A few years from now when this topic comes up, let's agree to laugh nervously and immediately change the subject," can sometimes be all it takes to give our brain the mental jolt it needs.

### Reward

In Chapter Four we saw the importance of rewarding success at work and celebrating small milestones. But when it comes to fighting stress at work, we also need to remember that a little fun can provide a boost when we need it the most. In those moments where you or your team are feeling overwhelmed to the point that you think you *can't possibly take a break from work for something fun*, that is *exactly* the time you need to take a break. Quite simply, you need to break before you break.

For example, search-and-rescue dogs will get demoralized and stop working if they're in a situation where they're only finding dead bodies. To keep up their spirits, rescue officials have been known to bury a live team member in the rubble so the dogs can experience the joy and reward of finding a live person. Hey, if it works with dogs....

In fact, it can work with humans exceptionally well. Attaching a positive reward to some of your recurring stressors can be an effective way to minimize their negative impact. Some businesses have offered a "Jerk of the Week" award to the employee who had to deal with the most obnoxious customer or client. One of my clients placed a bin full of chocolates in the middle of the office as a way of minimizing everyone's stress when a noisy train rumbled past—you were only allowed a chocolate when a train went by.

In one office I worked in we had the "bonehead play of the month" award. Everyone had to nominate themselves (it really doesn't build the whole team spirit thing if you start nominating each other), and at the end of every month the self-designated boneheads would vie for a reward. Not only did this help reduce the stress associated with the event, it encouraged everyone to discuss their mistakes so they weren't repeated.

Barry Williams, of Barney's Motel fame, extended this concept to his customers by starting a fly bounty after guests started grumbling about the presence of flies in the motel rooms. Williams put a fly swatter and humorous poster in each room advertising the bounty:

"Barney Hates Flies. So the Barnmeister says smack 'em if you got 'em. We pay $0.10 per fly you kill without marking our walls. Bring their filthy (uncrushed) carcasses to the office for your reward."

Once the bounty was in place, the customers stopped complaining.

There's no end to the humorous things you can reward in your workplace: Worst hair day, worst workday of the month award, biggest gaffe award, or commute from hell awards can all help give people a laugh when they need it most.

### Relax!

As we've seen, humor is an effective relaxant. It's also a triple threat in the fight against stress. Laughter helps us relax, even loosening our muscles in places where we carry a lot of tension. It's also a form of mental flossing—shifting us emotionally, even if just for a moment. And it can break the tension in a conflict situation by helping, as we saw in the previous chapter, to shift people from convergent to divergent thinking.

We all have stories of humor coming to the rescue in a tense situation—perhaps a staff meeting where someone says something so utterly unbelievably stupid that the oxygen disappears for a while, then something funny happens and it's like a breath of fresh air.

I saw the power of humor to relax people while aboard the worst flight of my life. The turbulence was so bad that several passengers were throwing up. This was not, as you might imagine, a fun day at the office for the flight attendant. Or for us, for that matter.

Once the turbulence subsided, the flight attendant—sensing our abject fear—did something remarkably effective to break the tension. She paused after cleaning up some vomit, shot her hands up into the air like a victorious Olympian, and yelled out: "God, I *love* my job!"

After a brief moment of silence, the plane filled with laughter. It was as though the oxygen masks had dropped, offering us a chance to breathe again. The laughter pushed out the fear. Facial expressions relaxed; people were smiling again. The message: If we can find the humor in *this*, maybe we're going to be okay.

Doing something that off-the-wall is sometimes what the stress doctor ordered. Getting on an elevator backward, skipping to your next meeting, blowing bubbles, juggling scarves, engaging in a Silly String battle, or getting up and announcing a "fun dance" party for three minutes might sound silly and if so, perfect! That's exactly what the humor doctor ordered.

As the research suggests, what matters most is that we take control of our own humor resources and practice more positive forms of self-enhancing and affiliative styles of humor. So you need to do something that suits your own personality, something that fits your own style of humor.

Since self-enhancing humor is largely about finding the funny in life's challenging situations, make sure you flex your funny bone on a regular basis. Treat your sense of humor like a muscle that requires constant conditioning and training.

Here are some simple ways to nurture your sense of humor and help you and your team create a more relaxed atmosphere in the face of stress:

- Starting the workday with a good attitude is essential, so encourage employees to share ideas on how to relax during their commute—perhaps listening to comedy instead of talk radio, or reading funny material on the train;
- Many hospitals have humor carts stockpiled with various humor resources to help patients and families relax, so why not create your own version of a hospital humor cart, stockpiling it with funny books, DVDs and props that will help haha-challenged people relax;
- Create a humor resources library and encourage people to contribute to it and make use of it;
- Create a humor First Aid kit for your team by having everyone contribute something to it;
- Digital Equipment, a computer manufacturer based in Colorado Springs, Colorado, has a "Grouch Patrol" that roams the workplace in search of grumps, presumably with the goal of de-grumpi-fying them;
- One of the most effective ways of growing your sense of humor is to practice looking for the unintentionally funny, such as those poorly written newspaper headlines ("Bridge Held Up By Red Tape," "Miners Refuse to Work After Death,"); or warning labels ("For Indoor or Outdoor Use Only,"); or signs ("Ears Pierced While You Wait," "Today Only, Bras Half Off,") so start a humor book or file where you encourage everyone to contribute their funny observations of accidental humor;
- An American bank holds "Laugh-in Luncheons" every Friday, wherein employees watch classic sitcoms;

- At Beryl, employees write down funny observations or funny things people have said or done at work and deposit them into a Laugh Box—whenever anyone needs a bit of a chuckle, they read a few entries out loud;
- Create a ritual to blow off steam and help people re-energize during the afternoon blahs—maybe a five-minute dance party, or a five-minute "silly hour" every day at 3 pm;
- As we've seen, watching sitcoms helps people relax before a stressful event. In fact, the baseball star Johnny Damon partially credits a comedy video for the Boston Red Sox's 2004 World Series victory. The team watched the comedy before playing and Damon said the laughter helped the players relax. So why not watch five minutes of clean comedy before a big sales pitch, presentation, or stressful day ahead?
- Create an online databank of comedy resources that employees can tap into during their off hours;
- Try some theater improv exercises to help people relax. A great exercise guaranteed to get everyone laughing and relaxed is the "energy ball," wherein people stand in a circle and pass an imaginary ball of energy to each other by clapping it out and catching it with a clap. It's simple and a surefire way to get everyone smiling;
- Create a "Fun Squad" of deputies that watches out for overstressed employees and is given the power to conduct a humor raid to help them relax;
- Encourage random acts of humor so that people will be surprised (in a good way) as they go throughout their workday. It could be as simple as leaving sticky notes with funny quotes or thoughts in random locations throughout the office, so people discover them serendipitously;
- Bring in a team of massage therapists to offer free shoulder massages as a way of saying thanks to employees during a particularly stressful time (no, this isn't a humor tip, but I guarantee people will be in better humor afterward!);

- Create an official Stress Busters Squad or Pet Peeve Patrol whose mission is to find sources of stress and come up with creative solutions to deal with them;
- Add a humor component to all your official health and wellness campaigns and fairs;
- Stressed workers in Stockholm enjoy the relaxation benefits of "Disco Lunches," where employees gather in different public places and dance their stress away. If disco isn't your thing (and I'm guessing it might not be for many of you), why not encourage something else to help employees blow out the cobwebs, laugh and get a bit of exercise over their lunch hour or coffee break?
- About 50% of Taiwanese workplaces have an official dog in residence and, according to the *Journal of Workplace Health Management*, this may be just what the stress doctor ordered. They found that the presence of dogs in the workplace lowers everyone's stress levels. A study from Central Michigan University also found that dogs at work increase cooperation, trust, team cohesion and intimacy between colleagues.[28]

I could go on, since there is no end to the ideas you could employ to reduce the stress temperature in your workplace. The key to success is to involve all the employees and ask people what will work for them to create a more relaxed environment. It's not going to be one or two things that will make the difference, and it will only work if you sustain the fun over the long run.

Having everyone wear a name tag on Friday featuring their "Superhero Alter-Ego" name, or celebrating "Third-Person Thursday" may seem trite and even a little silly, but simple gestures such as these can keep everyone smiling even during the busiest and most challenging days.

And of course, you'll want to keep everyone smiling if you want to laugh all the way to the bank. After all, happy, loyal, passionate employees create the environment for happy, loyal, passionate customers.

## Key Messages and Ideas

1. Stress costs more than you might think. Beyond the obvious symptoms associated with increased absenteeism, "presenteeism"—where employees aren't feeling fully engaged at work—might be costing you *far* more than you think.

2. Laughter may not be the *best* medicine, but it's an effective stress reducer and it has been associated with many health benefits.

3. All humor is not created equal. Some styles are healthier and more effective at combating stress than others. The most effective style is self-enhancing humor: Maintaining a humorous outlook on life, making funny observations and keeping a sense of humor in the face of adversity.

4. Although workplaces should foster an attitude that supports a positive humor style, black (or "gallows") humor can play a healthy role in helping people cope with stressful events at work.

5. Humor is a powerful re-framing tool that can help you choose a different reaction in a stressful event. You can train your inner voice to maintain a healthier, more positive perspective.

6. Tapping into some fun can serve as a positive reward in the face of stress.

7. Humor is a triple threat when it comes to fighting stress. Laughter relaxes you physically, shifts your thinking, and shifts you emotionally. There are hundreds of ways of tapping into your sense of humor to help you relax in the face of stress; the most effective will be the ones that match your personality and humor style.

8

# Humor as a Brand Advantage, Part Two—Attracting Customers Into the Fold

"More than any other element,
fun is the secret to Virgin's success."
– Sir Richard Branson

A common concern of many weary airline travelers is ending up next to a caterwauling infant for the duration of their flight. WestJet Airlines, a company renowned for good customer service, recognized a potentially huge competitive advantage and decided to do something about this growing concern by offering child-free cabins aboard select flights. It was a brilliant strategic move that demonstrated WestJet's responsiveness to its customers' needs and concern for their welfare.

The challenge, however, was how to accommodate the needs of families and get children safely to their destination? The solution: Kargo Kids. At check-in, the children would be carefully loaded into a "travel toboggan" (a playful renaming of plastic luggage bins used at airport security), where they would safely ride along the conveyer belt using the same route as the checked-in luggage, to be met by a friendly Kargo Kids counselor and unloaded into a special area of the airplane cargo hold that had been redesigned for the kids, complete with toys and a feeding trough. It was a classic win-win for everyone concerned: Business travelers, exhausted parents needing a little down time and, of course, the children, who were now free to run around and scream to their hearts content.

For an airline that has branded itself as customer-focused, family-friendly and fun, it was a home run. Especially since the program was announced on April Fool's Day.

The Kargo Kids program is just one of several April Fool's Day pranks pulled off by WestJet Airlines, topped only by its outrageous 2013 Christmas stunt. That's when passengers interacted with a virtual Santa Claus at a booth at their departure gate, where they were prompted to tell Santa what they wanted for Christmas. WestJet elves in Calgary—the customers' destination—immediately went to work, buying and wrapping the items. When the travelers landed in Calgary, they were dumbfounded to see freshly wrapped gifts sliding down the luggage belt in advance of their bags. The stunt garnered WestJet worldwide publicity, and the video retelling the story has earned more than thirty-six million views on YouTube and resulted in more than one hundred requests for interviews from the media.

WestJet's use of humor (nearly every Canadian can retell at least one groan-inducing joke told by one of their flight attendants) is a key reason the airline has been listed as the most-loved brand in their home province of Alberta, and the second-most-loved brand in Canada.

WestJet isn't the only company to strategically use humor to brand itself. As we saw in Chapter Two, numerous companies are making names for themselves as great places to work to attract and keep employees. But let's turn our attention to what ultimately matters: Customers. In fact, this entire book has been leading up to a fundamental, yet often-overlooked principle: Happy employees lead to happy customers. Treat your employees the way you'd expect your employees to treat your most passionate and loyal customers and chances are that's how they'll treat customers.

But before we turn our attention to some of the ways businesses are laughing all the way to the bank through their creative and fun approaches to customer service, let's look at what some companies are doing to attract customers in the first place by branding themselves as fun places to do business. Our starting point is another airline, one that has taken its approach to branding literally.

## BRANDING? IT'S EASY!

Established in 2001, South Africa's Kulula Airlines has definitely made its presence known. A low-frills discount airline (Kulula is from the Nguni languages of Zulu and Xhosa, meaning, "It's easy"),

Kulula strived to brand itself from the get-go as customer-friendly, easy-to-do-business-with and, above all, fun. What better way to brand yourself as a fun airline than by advertising it right on your planes? Kulula repainted one of their Boeing 737s in bright green with a massive white "Flying 101" label painted along the sides of the aircraft and numerous smaller labels pointing out the various parts of the plane, including labels such as:

- Sun roof;
- Big Cheese (captain, my captain!);
- Co-captain (the other pilot on the PA system);
- Our door is always open, unless we're at 41,000 feet;
- Stabilizer (the other steery thingy);
- The go-go juice.

Even the inside of the plane was playfully labeled: The overhead compartments became "VIP seating for your hand luggage," while the emergency exit was tagged "the throne zone." To further promote their fun brand, Kulula revamped an old-school 1976 Chrysler Special Edition to look like one of their airplanes complete with green color, playful labeling (the back seats are labeled "economy class"), drop-down oxygen masks, adjustable reading lights and an ejector seat. The car cruises around South African streets soliciting miles of smiles while strengthening their offbeat, friendly brand.

Other planes have been painted with cows, or in camouflage with the label "No one saw us coming," or with labels on both sides of the plane: "This end up."

All this literal branding reflects Kulula's corporate image, which embraces Great Fun as one of their six core values. They define Great Fun as: "We help people lighten up. Smiles and jokes are free. We always want to be genuinely friendly and provide the right environment for our staff's natural talent to shine."

To build a consistent image for what some have dubbed as "the most fun airline in the world," Kulula hires comedians as guest editors for each edition of their in-flight magazine. They also audition their own employees for roles in hilarious marketing videos, including a series called "Kulula Case Studies" where they outline cheeky marketing campaigns, including a Bollywood-style takeoff on the

Tom Cruise hit *Top Gun*, featuring a leather-clad Kulula employee on a Segway, rather than a motorcycle.

As with WestJet, Kulula takes advantage of every April Fool's Day to strengthen its playful brand with a fun announcement or prank, such as its "launch" into the skywriting business with their passenger jets, thanks to technological improvements that allow skywriting to become a seamless part of everyone's flying experience.

## GOING ALL THE WAY IS THE KEY—EVEN IF IT MEANS AIRING YOUR DIRTY LAUNDRY

The key to successful branding is to look for any and all opportunities to engage customers with a consistent message that reinforces the image you want to convey. Some companies have built a brand advantage that helps them stand out with a fun business name, such as:

- Jack the Clipper (London-based hair salon);
- Curl Up & Dye (hair salon);
- Frying Nemo (fish and chips shop);
- Life's a Cabernet (wine store);
- Tree Wise Men (landscapers);
- Pane in the Glass (window shop);
- Pulp Friction (paper recyclers);
- Indiana Bones Temple of Groom (doggy daycare boutique);
- Florist Gump (flower shop).

Of course some of the names are painfully corny and certain businesses do lend themselves to puns more than others. Some, like the Pi Bar in San Francisco, play up their name by offering happy hour between 3:14 pm and 6:28 pm each day featuring, naturally, a slice of cheese pie and the beer of the day for $6.28.

If hair salons are the undisputed champions of the punny business-naming world (and trust me, they are), wineries likely come a close second for the most creative and playful names.

The Dirty Laundry winery is one of my favorite wineries in British Columbia's Okanagan Valley. The name comes from an historic Summerland laundry that reportedly housed a brothel, earning it the nickname "Dirty Laundry." As with many of the wineries I've visited, names can matter—sometimes a lot. As I asked my fellow wine tourists what prompted their visit to different wineries, frequently the response was something to the effect of: "It was the name—we just *had* to see it!"

What I love about Dirty Laundry isn't just their fabulous wines, it's how they've built their fun brand into every aspect of their business. So the winery's logo features a red-hot iron with images of women in the steam; the tagline reads: "The Okanagan's Dirty Little Secret." Their newsletter is called Laundry Lines and their welcome sign resembles a giant sheet hanging on a clothesline. The entrance gate posts are giant clothes pegs. The tasting room and gift shop is reminiscent of an old-fashioned bordello (not that I'd know what one looks like) complete with lingerie strewn about the display cases. They sell products such as pink stiletto wine bottle holders. Of course their wine names include such gems as, "A Secret Affair," "Naughty Chardonnay," and "A Girl in Every Port." Even the descriptions of the wine are playfully suggestive.

*Everything* reinforces Dirty Laundry's fun image. Too many businesses make only a half-hearted attempt to weave a consistent story throughout their operation, thereby missing out on many golden opportunities, when the real dirty little secret to standing out from the herd with your brand is to, as the Dirty Laundry winery owners might suggest, go all the way.

## BE GRAND—NOT BLAND!

Some businesses have undoubtedly prospered at least in part from their clever name. The Vancouver-based company 1-800 Got Junk? is another prime example. Their slogan? "We'll stash your trash in a flash." Of course, unless you're a smaller enterprise or brand new start-up, changing your name isn't an option. The good news is that there are still plenty of opportunities to inject a bit of fun into your branding. It's just a matter of looking at every point of contact with your customers to see if there's an opportunity to inject some humor and ideally, some *relevant* humor that reinforces your name, product, service or values.

So if not a fun business name, a humorous slogan or sign is an easy starting point, such as these real-life examples:

"We repair what your husband fixed!" (plumbing truck);

"We really know our stuff!" (taxidermist's office);

"Time wounds all heels" (podiatrist's office);

"We're easy to get a lawn with" (turf farm);

"No appointment necessary—we hear you coming" (muffler shop);

"We run a shady business" (tarp business);

"Let us steer you in the right direction" (meat company);

"Get your buns in here!" (pastry shop);

"A good flush beats a full house" (plumbing);

"I only have ICE for you" (ice company);

"A great place to take a leak" (tire shop);

"If you don't see what you're looking for, you've come to the right place!" (optometrist's office).

Adding a slogan like one of these is a simple way to add some fun to your business cards as well. When people have an encounter with comedian Steve Martin, he hands them a business card with his signature on it that reads:

"This certifies that you have had a personal encounter with me and that you found me to be warm, polite, intelligent and funny." Steve Martin

Martin uses these cards to brand himself. In fact, he's blatantly telling you what his brand is! What a simple networking idea to adapt—and a great lesson in marketing, to boot.

Business cards aren't going the way of the dodo any time soon, so they are still an easy way to say something about your brand and help you connect at a personal level. Something fun can get people holding onto your cards and—more importantly—sharing them with other people.

If not a funny slogan, how about a fun personal photo, a humorous quote, a weird statistic, a photo of your dog... *something* that helps you stand out. How about putting everyone's personal bio on the back of the professional front? Or something even more creative that reinforces your business. Benton Brothers Fine Cheese of Vancouver, BC, has cards that resemble slices of Swiss cheese, replete with holes. Flow Yoga, also of Vancouver, boasts cards that resemble tiny yoga mats. An optometrist has a card with suspiciously small lettering, while a fitness trainer offers a rubber business card that you need to stretch before you can see his contact information. A sales company uses its business cards as referral cards, including a blank space where people can add their own name.

Adding a fun alternative job title or alternative superhero name is also a simple way to make a humorous impression. We've already met some real DIRTTbags, a Lead Culture Guide and a Director of First Impressions, but there's also the Manager of Vibe, a much more fun and meaningful job title for the food and beverage manager at the Peabody Hotel in Orlando. Or the Intergalactic Federation King Almighty and Commander of the Universe, the official title of the person who handles Google's space projects.

Names like Marketing Evangelist, Social Media Ninja and Chief Happiness Officer are becoming a bit trendy in some industries and yes, can come across as a tad cheesy and even cliché. But if you find a title that makes your customers smile, reinforces your image and describes the true nature and ultimate goal of a person's job, why wouldn't you use it?

## BIG ASS BRANDING IN CYBERSPACE

Business cards are still small potatoes compared to the real modern-day business card—your online presence. We've already seen how companies are using videos to sell themselves as great places to work, but what about your customers? What image are they left with after visiting your website? Are you conveying a customer-friendly presence that exudes warmth and a personal, human touch? Adding humor to your website can help humanize your company and soften your image, helping customers feel as though they are connecting with a real person and not an automated, sterile machine.

Kentucky's Big Ass Fans features a fair amount of edgy humor on its website, which is highly appropriate for them. After all, their name is Big Ass Fans... even though the ass they speak of is a donkey. So they embrace the controversy surrounding their name by including some of the hate mail they receive in a kudos section on their site. They even have a hilarious video that pokes fun at the whole controversy. (On a side note: If you're going to do something outrageous—like succeed the way Big Ass Fans has—you might upset some people, though perhaps you didn't want them as customers in the first place!)

Even more conservative businesses and industries are getting into the act. Recall that Integris Credit Union, who we met briefly in Chapter Two, uses their hilarious videos to help promote their brand and market their approach to phenomenal customer service. The employees come across as personable and charming and the videos do a masterful job of straddling the line between goofy humor and professionalism.

For most companies, humor isn't the main course being served up, it's merely the seasoning that can help connect your customers to your brand when they cruise around your website. As we saw with humor in advertising, the key is to be relevant. Here's a few simple ideas to ponder:

- A funny top-ten list that highlights the ten oddest requests you've had, or the ten most unusual ways people have used your product or service;
- A dedicated humor section where you share clean jokes or anecdotes related to your industry;
- A dedicated "Ask ______" column that answers inquiries in a very conversational and sometimes amusing manner;
- Fun before-and-after photos or videos showing your customers' reactions to your products or services;
- A video or blog series featuring your employees who answer readers' questions or offer additional tips and insights;
- A "Meet ______" section that introduces customers to your team in a fun, friendly manner;
- A "Don't Click Here" or "Super Cool Stuff That We Only Want Our Most Valuable Customers to Know About" button that sends customers to offbeat sections of your site or to a special promotional page;

- A "Day in the Life" video that shows off your company in a time-lapsed video;
- A contest or trivia section for your customers;
- A poll that asks quirky questions related to your product or service, keeping in mind that, as with employee engagement, anything that involves your customers or draws them into a conversation will increase the likelihood of true engagement;
- A customer Hall of Fame where you highlight great customer responses and special awards or rewards that you grant to your customers.

Part of any online presence includes social media. From YouTube channels to business Facebook pages, from Tumblr to Twitter, social media is the wild west of marketing, especially when you factor in how best to use humor. There are thousands of success stories and thousands of social media derailments due to humor. Some companies have had great success setting up Twitter accounts that represent their mascot or a product; others have suffered an epic Twitter backlash because an employee tweeted an offensive comment in a lame attempt at being funny.

The annual Shorty Awards honor personalities, companies and brands that have created highly successful social media campaigns. One finalist, Zzzquil, demonstrated just how effective a platform such as Twitter can be if done correctly. After discovering people were already talking about their product on social media—especially at night when insomnia struck—they decided to dive in with a Twitter account that focused on bringing humor and warmth to a topic that was typically handled in a sterile, medicinal way. The result: More than sixteen million online impressions.

After learning that 40% of young adults admitted to using social media in the bathroom, Charmin toilet paper found tremendous success using a little potty humor on their Twitter account #Tweetfromtheseat. Their Twitter presence earned Charmin accolades from numerous media outlets, including *Time* magazine, which called Charmin the "Sassiest Brand on Twitter."

Even older, more staid organizations have found success using humor in social media—eighty-five-year-old Delta Airlines maintained its brand image while using witty tweets to increase their followers by 50%. One of the most re-tweeted tweets: "Baby got back! We like big jets and we cannot lie, this 737 is ready to fly!"

Heck, even the CIA used humor in their very first tweet in June 2014: "We can neither confirm nor deny that this is our first tweet."

This topic really is an entire book unto itself, so let me just offer a few thoughts here:

- Humor can help your video go viral. But it needs to be congruent with your branding; it should be carefully planned and executed; it shouldn't come across as a sales ad; and it needs to be part of a broader marketing and branding plan. So always consider the context: Why are you doing the video and what are you hoping to achieve?
- You need to stay clear of jokes and keep the humor as safe as possible (unless you're trying to be edgy and are prepared for some backlash). It's not necessarily about being witty, it's a conversation, a connection;
- Social media is a reminder that no matter what you do, you can't control the story of your brand alone—it's a co-authorship and work in progress that includes contributions from everyone who is saying things about your company, products and services online. Don't fear this; embrace it.

Embracing contributions from beyond your company means that companies sometimes need to have a thick skin and to be able to laugh at their own brand. For example, the NBC sitcom *30 Rock* spent seven years poking fun at General Electric, NBC's parent company. Tina Fey's character continually mocked GE's "Six-Sigma" productivity culture, while Alex Baldwin's character often portrayed a GE executive that some companies might want to distance themselves from.

So were GE executives cringing every time an episode of *30 Rock* aired? Hardly. Not only were they in on the joke from the beginning, they even went so far as to air a series of TV ads thanking *30 Rock* for all the laughs over the years, and they created a "Favorite Moments" page on the show's official website.

As GE and many others have proven, just because your company is in a serious business doesn't mean your social media presence needs to always be staid. Injecting some humor into social media is a great way to stand out from the herd, add some personality to your brand, and connect with customers at a human level.

## WHO WOULDN'T LISTEN TO A PIRATE?

Another often-overlooked point of contact is the phone. Customer complaints about poor phone service are legion these days, from waiting an eternity to having to navigate a labyrinth of voice mail options only to be put on hold again, only to be told to start all over until you talk to someone who may or may not be located where you need them to be located. But of course, as these businesses remind us, "Your call is important to us!"

If your customers' calls truly are important to you (and they should be), make sure you are putting your best voice forward. Anyone who answers your phone in your organization is a Director of First Impressions and, as we all know, first impressions last.

Which is why Zappos puts a huge emphasis on its customer service training and coaching to ensure their employees make exceptional impressions over the phone. As an online retailer offering 24/7 call center support, phone support is key to Zappos' success. But it's also their primary vehicle for developing relationships with customers and building their brand. So although Zappos briefly considered outsourcing their call center overseas, they believed in a key principle of success: Never outsource your core competency.

This means their employees aren't given a script, the way many call center employees are. Why? Because Zappos wants its employees to come across as authentic human beings. They want employees to be themselves, share their natural sense of humor, and build a relationship with their customers.

Which isn't to say they are free to tell the latest "A priest, a rabbi and a kangaroo walk into the bar..." joke. Employees are trained extensively. They receive one-on-one coaching and feedback. All employees, regardless of where they end up in the company, spend the first four weeks in the same new hire training, which includes learning how to answer phones to reinforce their focus on service. Above all else they are encouraged (and trusted) to engage the customer in a human—and whenever possible—fun way. One employee

I met told me how he challenged himself to answer the phone in a different way for an entire day—making it fun for him and the customers. And one day over the Christmas season Zappos employees held a contest to see who could get the most customers to sing a Christmas carol.

Because Zappos understands that the most important goal is to build trust and relationships with their clients, they don't measure the quantity of calls employees field, the way many companies do. Instead, Zappos focuses on quality. They never upsell and if they don't stock a particular product that a customer is calling about, they'll happily recommend a competitor to them. Why? Because Zappos is playing the long game. Although most of their calls are short and sweet, their record length for a call is over ten hours. The marathon call was with a very lonely person who needed a human connection. Because of Zappos phenomenal culture of caring, the employee understood that engaging that customer mattered.

What if you can't have a Director of First Impressions answering your phones? The next best thing you can do is to add some fun to your voice mail system. CXtec, a telecommunications company based in Syracuse, New York, has been listed as one of the best places to work in the US. They embrace the philosophy "Work hard, play hard" and they "have fun doing serious business." That brand comes through when you phone their offices. Although you are listening to a recorded voice mail message, the voice is enthusiastic, warm and conversational. More importantly, they've included some fun, offering callers options such as:

- If you know how to spell your party's name, your smarts will be rewarded by pressing six;
- For the best sales team in the land, press one;
- For customer service that rocks, press two;
- To hear a rocking clip from our house band the Dinosaurs, press seven;
- To hear a pretty funny joke, press eight;
- If you're not sick of my voice and you need the options again, press nine.

Simple, yet effective. Why offer up customer support in a bland, monotone voice, when you can enthusiastically announce customer service that *rocks*?

The online photo-sharing site Shutterfly offers customers the usual array of options on its customer support line, with one notable and hilarious exception. After hearing the menu, they offer a pirate version: "Ahoy matey, draw tight for here be your options..." and then everything is converted into pirate-ese. Who *wouldn't* choose the pirate option? How could you not leave that call smiling and thinking that Shutterfly is a fun place to do business?

## EVEN SERIOUS BRANDS CAN MARCH TO A DIFFERENT DRUMMER

Some of you may be thinking, "That's fine for *those* companies, but that could never work where I work because our brand is very high class and we cater to a very serious clientele."

Fair enough. As I've mentioned, the key to effective branding is to be congruent with your image. Some companies can get away with an edgy Big Ass rap song video or pirate voice mail option, others... not so much. But this doesn't mean there isn't room for any humor. Especially since all I'm really talking about is adding a human voice to your branding efforts and making a human connection with people. No matter how serious your business or how serious you think your customers are, there's *always* a little room for some safe humor.

In fact, many brands that might appear to be above all that "embracing fun" nonsense have reaped tremendous benefits with a bit of wackiness. Or, should I say, quackiness?

The Peabody Hotel in Memphis, Tennessee is a grand, elegant, historic hotel that caters to the rich and famous. It's the place to stay when in Memphis, even, evidently, if you're a duck. Despite its classy clientele and elegant architecture, the Peabody is home to the world-famous March of the Ducks, a tradition that dates back to 1933. Every morning at 11 am, an official and elegant Duckmaster leads a family of ducks from the rooftop, down the elevators and along a red carpet that leads to the historic fountain inside the grand hotel. The ducks spend the day in the fountain until their 5 pm checkout, when the

Duckmaster returns to lead the family back up to their penthouse suite for the evening.

When I visited the hotel the entire lobby, surrounding balconies and restaurant adjacent to the fountain were packed to the gills with curious paparazzi hoping to get a glimpse of the famous webbed celebrities. I talked to one woman who had convinced her husband to drive three hours out of their way on their cross-country road trip to take in the spectacle, which lasts all of five minutes.

As with the Dirty Laundry winery, the Peabody Hotel embraces its theme throughout the building with duck-shaped bars of soap in the hotel rooms and stuffed ducks for sale at their gift shop. The story of the march is presented on their website, the restaurant makes a point of telling you they don't serve duck, and there's even a duck walk of fame on their sidewalk featuring, you guessed it, duck prints.

The March of the Ducks is not only an example of a classy brand embracing a very unconventional tradition, it's also a reminder that marching to your own duck can help attract free media attention and publicity. Celebrities galore have dropped in to watch the march or have served as Honorary Duckmasters. The ducks have been featured on the *Tonight Show with Johnny Carson, Oprah Winfrey, Sesame Street,* served as a backdrop for a *Sports Illustrated* swimsuit shoot, been an answer to a question on *Jeopardy!* and are featured in a *Trivial Pursuit* board game question. So even if humor isn't part of your everyday playbook (although I hope that by now you are convinced it ought to be!), creating an outrageous tradition, contest, or promotional offer can help you attract free advertising and word-of-mouth publicity.

Vancouver's Eccotique Spa garnered free publicity across Canada with its "Confess and De-stress Spa Package," offered to anyone who participated in the heinous Vancouver riots following the Vancouver Canucks' defeat in the 2011 Stanley Cup final at the hands of the Boston Bruins. The offer was this: Come into one of our spas, sign a confession, get fingerprinted, and enjoy a day relaxing at the spa for free.

Did anyone take them up on their offer? No. Does it matter? Of course not. The story got picked up in newspapers from coast to coast.

Of course, most businesses recognize that putting people in seats is the name of the game. Especially when your game is baseball and you are literally trying to put people in your seats. One of the masters of doing just that is the St. Paul Saints baseball organization. One of their most outrageous gimmicks? Mime-o-vision. Since they don't have a jumbo screen to show instant replays, they hired mimes during one game to recreate the instant replays. From Tonya Harding nights to Enron-theme nights (where the scores were "adjusted") the organization is passionate about having fun and often uses outrageous themes (I mean seriously, who does a Tonya Harding or Enron theme?) and promotions to fill the seats and promote their fan-friendly organization.

Calgary's Big Rock Brewery not only generates free publicity with a fun annual tradition, they enlist their customers' help in creating fun ads for their beer products with their annual "Eddie Awards," which offer prizes for the most creative (and usually funniest) one-minute amateur ads. The event has morphed into a gala where finalists are screened and winners announced. The finalists are even dropped off in front of the theater by limo, where they get to walk the red carpet while paparazzi (played by local journalism students) take their photos and fire questions at them.

Whether it's a fun business name, slogan, sign, online presence, phone message, or heck, even a badge on your front-line employees' shirts reading "This End Up" (which I once encountered visiting a pharmacist), do an audit of your business to look for all opportunities to engage people with a bit of humor.

Of course, just as we saw earlier when it comes to employees, branding your business and attracting customers is only part of the job. All the branding in the world will only be window dressing if you don't look for ways to turn your customers into lifelong, passionate, enthusiastic fans for your business. It definitely won't sustain success unless you embrace the idea (as we're about to discover) that everything is customer service and customer service is everything.

## Key Messages and Ideas

1. Humor can be an important tool to brand yourself as a lovable or at least an attractive business to your customers.
2. The key to effective branding is to present a consistent image throughout every aspect of your operation.

3. There are numerous simple places to add some humor to help brand your business including your name, slogan, business cards, website, social media presence and over your phone.
4. Embracing humor in your brand means, at times, being able to laugh at your own company image.
5. Even more serious businesses can use humor in their branding. It's about first and foremost being authentic and adding a little heart and humanity.
6. Outrageous promotions and events can not only help you attract customers, they can help you attract free publicity and media attention.
7. All the branding in the world will be window dressing if it isn't backed up by phenomenal customer service that reinforces the brand.

# 9

# Turning Customers Into Raving Fans

"To WOW, you must differentiate yourself, which means do something a little unconventional and innovative. You must do something that's above and beyond what's expected."
– Tony Hsieh, CEO Zappos

I had an enlightening conversation with Siri a while back, one that reminded me of some key principles about memorable customer service. While waiting to board a flight to Toronto, I picked up my spanking new iPhone and asked Siri (and yes, I am on a first-name basis with my favorite voice recognition app), "Who's on first?"

Her response: "Yes, that's correct."

I couldn't believe it! Siri knew the classic Abbott and Costello vaudevillian baseball routine! Curious now, I then asked Siri why the chicken crossed the road. Her response: "Whether the chicken crossed the road or the road crossed the chicken depends on your frame of reference, according to Einstein."

Fair enough, I thought. But let's see how Siri handles the following timeless stumper: "How much wood could a woodchuck chuck if a woodchuck could chuck wood?"

Siri's response: "Well, since a woodchuck is really a groundhog, the correct question would be: How many pounds in a groundhog's mound when a groundhog pounds hog mounds?" This proved to be just one of more than a dozen humorous retorts to the woodchuck question.

So what, exactly, does this have to do with the humor advantage and inspiring customer service?

First, I think it should serve as a wake-up call to all humanity, especially those on the front lines of customer service. My mobile phone had just revealed a sense of humor—something none of the airline employees I had encountered that morning managed to do (I wasn't flying WestJet that day).

Secondly, Siri's response surprised me. In a good way. And isn't that one of the goals of great service—to surprise and delight the people we're trying to serve?

Lastly, but perhaps most importantly, Siri's humorous responses show that someone at Apple anticipated that some goofball like me was going to ask Siri those questions. Isn't anticipating the future needs of our customers—even before they need them—a hallmark characteristic of phenomenal customer service? (Or for that matter, inspiring leadership?)

## STOP PROVIDING GOOD CUSTOMER SERVICE!

Great organizations understand that there's a difference between long-term customers and loyal, raving fans that will serve as ambassadors for your business. Zappos has a fantastic mantra that every business interested in converting customers into raving fans should adopt: "We are in the service business, we just happen to sell shoes." What a great way for everyone to view their work: "I am in the service business, I just happen to______________________."

This attitude needs to be adopted by every employee in your business, from your CEO to front-line staff, from your sales reps to IT experts. It needs to be embraced as a passionate calling, and championed as your call to action.

Furthermore, you need to broaden the definition of customer service in a couple ways. First, relentlessly remind all your employees that everything they do—even when they don't have front-line contact with customers—still impacts the service you ultimately provide.

More than that, great cultures are built when people remember that everyone they interact with at work is one of their customers. If you're a leader, your customers are your employees and you need to treat them with the same dedicated passion as you'd want your front-line employees treating your customers. If you're an employee, your boss is one of your customers and so are all your colleagues. In fact, one simple but effective definition of teamwork is offering great customer service to the rest of one's teammates.

Imagine how work might change if everyone wholeheartedly embraced that concept.

Then you need to broaden the definition of service and remind everyone that service isn't just about those sometimes-brief moments of contact with customers. It's about how easy your website and voice mail system is to navigate, how clean and welcoming your facilities are, being open five minutes before you're supposed to be, and how you listen and communicate. It's about responsiveness, but more importantly (as Siri reminds us), it's anticipating the needs of your customers.

You need to, above all else, stop offering *good* customer service.

Let me restate it in caps, so you think I'm yelling at you (which I sort of am, but in a friendly way): STOP OFFERING GOOD CUSTOMER SERVICE!

Why? Because your customers already *expect* good customer service. They expect your facilities will be open when they're supposed to be, the place will be clean, and employees will be friendly and responsive.

So all you're doing by providing good customer service is *meeting expectations*. You're merely staying out of the customer service dog house.

But you don't turn customers into loyal fans by merely meeting expectations. Nobody ever says, "Wow, we need to go back there again because everything was, um, well, adequate and I got exactly what I expected I would!"

With that in mind, there are two things you need to do to truly make an impression. Not surprisingly, these two things can be helped along immensely with a bit of humor and fun:

1. Exceed people's expectations of good service.

2. Be different than everyone else. Stand out from the herd to be heard. Shatter the stereotypes surrounding your industry by asking how you can be "un__________?"

That's it. It's not fancy; it's not rocket science. But it *is* the key to success. For this approach to take root in your organization, you need to embrace a culture-wide approach. You need to hire, train, coach and mentor with a service attitude in mind. Leaders need to relentlessly model what they expect to see in others and relentlessly communicate the importance of service, starting by ensuring everyone understands why it matters.

Here are five reasons why service matters now, more than ever.

1. It's what you do. Service is your entire raison d'être. The *only* reason you exist is to provide a service to your customers, and every employee needs to embrace that concept every time they become the Director of First Impressions. In a business environment where you can't control the cost of your raw materials or what your competition is going to do next or what's going to happen to the currency rate or the weather or you name it, the one thing you *can* control is how well you deliver service. Just like creating an inspiring workplace culture, offering phenomenal service can become one of your top competitive advantages.

2. Focusing on exceptional service as one of your overriding values can lead to other workplace improvements: A safer work environment, cost efficiencies, improved communication, enhanced teamwork, reduced silos and more innovation. When everyone clearly understands their primary purpose, an entire culture can be transformed. One more time: There's a chicken-and-egg relationship. When everyone provides phenomenal service, your culture can't help but improve. Conversely, improve your culture and the desire to offer great service becomes a natural byproduct.

3. If you *don't* provide great service, people will talk. Not like they did in the olden days of say, the 1990s, where they might have gone home and shared their story with a dozen or so friends and family members. Nowadays they'll spread the word before they've even left your premises. They'll tweet their disgust while in the lineup or sitting on the tarmac or lounging in the lobby of your hotel. Those tweets will get re-tweeted to another 47,326 people.

   Or they'll post it on their Facebook page and create a feeding frenzy of similar tales of woe that their friends are dying to get off their chests. Or they'll blog about it. Or they'll upload a photo to Instagram. Or they'll get their eleven-year-old to create a www.WeHateYou.com website. They'll vent a spleen on Trip Advisor or yell for help on Yelp. Or, they'll vent in a YouTube video in such a hilarious, outrageous way that the video will go viral.

That's right—they'll use the humor advantage against you.

Remember Dave Carroll's "United Breaks Guitars" story from Chapter Five and how his story touched over *one hundred million people worldwide*? He could have been singing about you. Every one of your employees need to recall the old TV classic, *Candid Camera,* because these days, your entire business is on candid camera.

4. Provide outrageously unique customer service and people will talk. But not like in the olden days, of say, the 1990s, when they might have shared their story with a dozen or so friends and family members. No, now they'll take a photo of your hilarious sign or slogan and upload it to Facebook or Twitter before they've left the premises. They'll take a "selfie" in front of your funny business sign and then rave about the exceptional service. They'll sing your praises on LinkedIn, Trip Advisor, Yelp and a dozen other social media sites.

   Here's my belief, supported by informal surveys on my own social media sites and with my own postings: People are far more likely to talk about you in social media if you do something outrageous or demonstrate a sense of humor. Yes, people will comment when they've received great service as well, but not to the degree they will when they've experienced something fun and different. The message is far more likely to be shared and re-shared and re-shared again when it's something outrageous, clever, or funny.

   Consider how readily people upload videos of their hilarious flight attendant's safety announcement and how much these videos get viewed and shared. One video of a Southwest Airlines flight attendant who received a rousing round of applause for her outrageously funny safety announcement ("Position your seatbelt tight and low across the hips like my grandmother wears her support bra") went immediately viral, attracting more than eleven million views in one week.

5. Last, but surely not least, it's *fun* to provide exceptional service. So as much as businesses need to take to heart that happy employees create happy customers, the reverse is also true. Happy customers make for more happy employees. Happy customers make employees feel good about their jobs. Happy customers cause less strife and conflict. Doing something great for a customer is powerfully rewarding. Recall Pike's Place fish market's desired customer service goal of "making someone's day," and how a simple shift in thinking can create a more positive experience for everyone concerned. Allowing employees the freedom to make someone's day also frees them up to think for themselves, to be more creative, and to bring their personality along for the ride.

   A study undertaken by Sears found that if their employees' attitudes improved by 5% (as measured by ten different factors, including how their bosses treated them), customer satisfaction rose by 1.3% and profits by 0.5%.[1] Those might not sound like huge numbers, but in a large corporation they add up. Consider the potential impact of improving employee attitudes by 50%! Ideally, you want to create a positive feedback loop, where happy employees create happier customers, who in turn create even happier employees... and so on.

   When I asked employees at Zappos if they ever experienced stress, one front-line employee responded, "Yes, but it's a positive kind of stress. It's fun stress. In my former customer service jobs I got stressed out having to explain why we couldn't do something, or why something was against our policy. Here, I am empowered to always find a way to say yes, instead of always saying no. And that's fun!"

We tend to focus on the impact that a phenomenal customer service gesture has on our customers, but we forget that it also has a long-lasting, positive impact on employees as well. If you want to add more fun to your workplace and create an inspiring culture, adding more fun and humor to your customers' lives is one of the best places to start.

## HE WHO LAUGHS LAST... BUYS MORE?

It's great getting customers to sing your praises, but what about getting them to open their wallets more often... or wider?

A study by Karen O'Quin and Joel Aronoff found that a bit of humor can influence people to pay more during negotiations.[2] In the study, participants had to negotiate with a seller over the purchase price of a painting. The seller made a final sales offer in one of two ways. Half the time the seller said he'd accept $6,000, the other half of the time he gave the same final offer, but this time he added a little humor by offering to throw in his pet frog. The impact of a little humor had a huge effect. Regardless of gender and regardless of the degree to which the seller's final price was above the amount originally offered, would-be buyers made a much greater compromise when offered the pet frog. So, either everyone in the study had a ten-year-old boy at home or, more likely, the humorous aside helped relax the buyers and put them in a more generous frame of mind.

Another study by humor researcher Dr. Paul McGhee found that when a salesperson used more humor, the buyer was willing to pay a higher price.[3] The study found that humor helped break down initial objections the buyers may have had and helped create an emotional bond with the seller, product or idea.

And a study described in the book, *Yes! 50 Scientifically Proven Ways to Be More Persuasive*, by Steven J. Martin, showed that simply sending a funny, inoffensive cartoon to the person you are negotiating with generated higher levels of trust and led to 15% larger profits.[4] Recipients of the funny cartoon were more than twice as likely as those who didn't receive the cartoon to make an opening offer that was deemed acceptable. The use of cartoons even resulted in shorter, more efficient negotiating time.

Legendary adman David Ogilvy once said, "All the world may love a clown, but nobody buys from one." Fair enough. I'm not sure I'd want to buy my next big-ticket item from a clown, either. But as any veteran salesperson knows, selling is all about relationship building. It's about making a personal connection and establishing trust. As we've seen throughout our journey, positive humor can help break the ice, soften our image, humanize us and strengthen trust. So although coming across like the office clown may not be the best approach, teaching your salespeople and front-line employees to use humor safely may pay off more than you might think.

## OUTSTANDING SERVICE THAT STANDS OUT

While we waited for a few late-transferring passengers, the WestJet flight attendant pulled out a flute and started performing over the PA system, offering up prizes for whoever was the first to guess the title of the song. A few passengers raised their hands over their heads and started swaying as though they were at a concert; everyone applauded and cheered when she was done.

Then the pilot (whose name has been changed for the simple reason that I can't remember) came on with a rather unusual announcement: "This is Captain Bob Roberts speaking. Uh... I don't sound very good. I'll be right back." Perplexed passengers laughed and looked puzzlingly at each other, I'm sure thinking the same thought as me: "Be right back? Aren't you sort of an integral part of the process, Bob?"

Moments later, though, he was back on the PA: "Ahh, I just had my second cup of coffee. That's better. *This*, my esteemed passengers, is Captain Roberts, the world's most handsome pilot. We are about to take this plane up to 36,000 feet where only the angels soar." He carried on with one of the funniest pilot announcements I've ever heard, earning an enthusiastic round of applause from appreciative passengers.

The flight attendant then announced that a couple was celebrating their twenty-fifth wedding anniversary and had been moved to business class. WestJet, at the time, had no business class.

More applause, more laughter.

At cruising altitude, the flight attendants handed out rolls of toilet paper to the front row of passengers, the object being that they had to unspool the rolls over their shoulders to the passengers behind them, racing the other side of the plane. The incentive? The winning side would be the first to be let off.

The laughter rose up again upon landing, as this just happened to be annual Nerd Day and the grounds crew members were all dressed as nerds.

This flight took place well before the days of social media, but do you think there's anyone aboard that flight who would not have relayed that story over and over? Combining a bit of fun in tandem with outstanding service gets you noticed. It gets you talked about. It strengthens your brand image. It builds up goodwill capital that you can withdraw from the bank the next time you need to make amends with a customer, as even the most stellar businesses do from time to time. It helps you stand out, exceed expectations and surprise your customers.

The Third Street Bakery in Phillipsburg, Kansas understands the power of goofy humor to get you noticed. The bakery is reputedly home of the largest chocolate donut in the US, what is affectionately known as the "Big Chocolate Honker." When someone orders the Honker, an employee honks an old-fashioned bike horn which then leads everyone—often including the customers who hang out in the bakery—to raise their arms in the air and yell out a boisterous "Honk! Honk!" That silly ritual has garnered the donut shop free publicity from news media in all the surrounding states.

No, it doesn't mean always turning your customer service into an "experience." Some of your customers don't care about having an experience. They want efficiency. They just want to get whatever it is they need and be on their way. But this doesn't, for a moment, discount the importance of offering a human connection, exceeding expectations and being a bit different... so you're memorable.

The good news is that it doesn't take much to exceed expectations, especially these days when people decry the lack of basic customer service. It all starts with attitude.

I was on a two-week fitness kick many years ago. Determined not to fall off the bandwagon, I headed out to the hotel fitness center. Unsure where to go, I stopped the first employee I encountered, a cleaning lady who looked like she was well past standard retirement age. After asking her where the fitness facility was, she responded with the most flirtatious smile I've seen in quite some time, poked me in the stomach and shook her head, saying, "You don't need a fitness facility, honey." I laughed out loud, thanked her for the compliment, and asked her if she would mind phoning my wife.

But my encounter wasn't over. This fabulous woman insisted on walking me to the gym and engaged me in the most enthusiastically thoughtful manner I could imagine en route, asking about my stay, my family and whether I've tried the clubhouse sandwich at the deli across the street. Wowed by her charm and sense of humor, I asked her if the hotel was a great place to work.

"Not really, no," was her unexpected response.

"Why are you so darn happy then?" I asked, genuinely wanting to know the answer.

Her response left me laughing: "When I'm like this the days go by twice as fast, I get huge honking tips, and when I have a favor to ask one of my colleagues, or my supervisor, guess what they always say?" Then, while sweeping her hands up and down both sides of her body, she smiled devilishly and said, "No one can turn *this* down."

Okay, time for a cliché alert. We don't do business with other businesses, we do business with other human beings. As an extremely busy international business speaker, I spend a lot of time in hotels. For the most part, a hotel is a hotel is a hotel. Yes, some have nicer features than others. But on balance, it's the people that sets them apart. Although I don't remember the woman's name, I do know this: She gave that hotel a soul, a personality, a beating heart. She, and she alone, made it memorable for me, thanks to her infectious, humorous attitude.

## THE EXTRA INCH, THE EXTRA MILE

To help ensure that employees are always focused on inspiring customer service, recognize and reward employees who offer ideas for going the extra inch and mile with your customer service.

Recognizing the extra-inch ideas and efforts is important because we often tend to focus on the big stuff, forgetting that customer service is really a game of inches. It's the small gestures that can make a difference with exceeding expectations and standing out; it's the small things that will upset your customers.

Focusing on the extra-inch stuff also encourages a mindset of continuous improvement and growth by encouraging people to keep thinking about the simple things that won't cost a lot of money or take a lot of extra time, but will still make a difference to your customers.

Consider my experience arriving at the Omega car rentals desk in New Zealand, where the front-counter employee offered us hot beverages, showed us on a map where we needed to go, loaded our luggage into the car, showed us how to adjust the seats, mirrors and radio, and waved good-bye to us as we drove off… all relatively small gestures, but combined, they left a lasting and powerful impression.

Jet Star airlines offers employees a chance to win one of three $500 prizes. To enter the draw, however, you need to submit an idea on how to improve customer service. Making the contest a lottery makes it fun to submit ideas, and not linking the suggestions *directly* to a financial reward eliminates the tricky proposition of incentivizing creative ideas, which as we saw, doesn't always work.

But you also need to recognize and celebrate the "hit it out of the ballpark" and the "go the extra mile" moments: Those epic gestures that you won't be able to do on a regular basis but where somebody does something so outrageously beyond the norm that even the media or people like me stand up and notice—and talk about it. Just like the story of Joshie, the stuffed giraffe.

Joshie, you see, was left behind at the Amelia Island (Florida) Ritz-Carlton by Chris Hurn's son, who was devastated at the loss of his prized stuffed giraffe. To ease the distress, Chris told his son that Joshie was fine, he had simply decided to extend his holiday. That same night, the Ritz-Carlton phoned to tell the Hurn family that Joshie had been found. To keep up the little white lie, Chris asked the person on the phone if he could take a photo of Joshie enjoying himself by the pool.

When Joshie arrived safe and sound back at the Hurn home, he didn't come with just one photo, however. The Ritz-Carlton included a package of fun goodies and an entire photo album showing Joshie enjoying himself throughout the hotel, including one showing Joshie relaxing at the spa.

Now *that's* a home-run customer service moment. Sure, it will likely turn just about any customer into a raving, obsessive fan of the business. But think about the impact it has on employees as well. The Joshie episode likely made someone's month, if not their year.

But here's the deal. There's no customer service manual on the planet that will say: "If a guest leaves a stuffed animal at your property, please create a photo album of said stuffed animal's adventures." You can't create a policy that generates moments like these, you need to build a culture that encourages epic stories and allows employees the creative freedom to jump on opportunities and go the extra mile in spectacular fashion.

When things occasionally go off the rails and you need to make amends with a customer, that's the time to *make sure* you go the extra mile, just like Johnson & Johnson did with its *Triple Sorry* apology video. Remember, some of your most loyal customers are the ones who have had a bad experience turned around by a huge gesture.

Whether you go the extra inch or the extra mile, just make sure your service continuously moves in the right direction. Identify potential weaknesses by asking your customers what *isn't* fun about doing business with you. Look for opportunities by tapping into the creativity of all your employees, partners, suppliers and customers. Build it into your culture with the VCR approach:

> **V**isible. Create a constant visual reminder of the need for everyone to adopt a service-first approach. A fun mascot, badges, buttons, signs, posters on the back of washroom stall doors... whatever it takes to keep the message front and center in the hearts and minds of every employee. Keep an empty seat or use a mannequin to represent the customer in all your meetings.
>
> **C**ommunicate. Keep the message alive. Share success stories from within and outside your organization. Open meetings with a service moment. Create a special section on your intranet site, newsletter or weekly emails to highlight a story.
>
> **R**ecognize and reward success. Turn your service champions into heroes. Celebrate successes. Create a wall of customer service fame, or keep a scrapbook and public display that highlights success moments and accolades from your customers.

## UPPING THE FUN FACTOR WITH YOUR CUSTOMERS

You've already read dozens of ideas, but here are a few more to get your creative juices flowing and to help you serve up more fun to your customers:

- Great service isn't about blindly smiling at the customer, it's doing something that gets the customer smiling back at you. The smiles you generate are the ones that truly matter, which is why I love the STP program initiative that Barry Williams, who we met earlier on, instituted with his employees. STP—Smile Transfer Protocol—was simple, yet remarkably effective. Each employee recorded the number of times they were able to transfer a smile onto a customer's face. The employee who created the most smiles at the end of the week won a prize. Williams said the impact on employee morale and customer satisfaction was phenomenal;

- Add some humor to your customer comment forms. Barry Williams found that when he added some humor to Barney's customer comment forms the response rate more than doubled;
- Have front-line employees wear a fun badge, like the "This End Up" pharmacist, that gives people a smile. Perhaps a badge with a fun slogan, service promise or quirky question;
- Slip a funny thought of the day, humorous quote, or clean joke into their bag when they purchase something;
- Thank your customers in an outrageous way: AFA JCDecaux sends a "hugging squad" over to a client's office when they are awarded a large contract;
- Find an offbeat way to say yes. When a customer asked a sales rep at AFA JCDecaux if they could do better on the price, the agent invited the customer to their games room and challenged him to a game of foosball with the offer being that for every point the sales rep scores they'll knock 1% off the price; for every point the customer scores they'll knock 2% off the price;
- To help bank-goers enjoy their banking experience, each branch of Umpqua Banks in Oregon is given a special fund designed solely to engage customers in a fun way. They've been known to bring in ice cream, popcorn and sandwich trucks for their customers;
- Have a rotating position in charge of greeting customers in a welcoming, fun way;
- Create a fun, unique space for your customers. The Winnipeg International Airport has an official "Hugging Rug" at the

bottom of the arrivals escalator, while the international airport in Nice, France offers a "Kiss 'n' Ride" commuter lane;

- Offer a wacky promotion: Gary's Uptown Restaurant in northern California offers a "Bald Guy's Menu" (the owner just happens to be bald) every Wednesday that attracts customers from more than fifty miles away. Customers pay based on how much hair they have: Totally bald and you pay nothing; half bald and you get a 50% discount. Men with toupees or comb-overs have to reveal their bald spots to qualify for the proportional discount. You can extend an idea like this to all sorts of offbeat promotions. A special left-handers' day discount, a full moon howl of a deal day, or "Ginger Day," where redheads get 20% off;

- In the 1920s advertisers would try to promote their clients' products by warning consumers of the dangers of afflictions such as Accelerator Toe, Vacation Knees and Office Hips. All fictitious maladies, of course. So why not invent some obviously exaggerated fake ailments your particular customers might be suffering from?

- We talked about how Google has some internal terms they use, such as Googliness, that help strengthen their culture. Why not extend this to your customers when possible and create some fun terms that tie into your name or brand?

- Instead of asking customers the standard pat questions that often feel scripted, ask quirky questions that will perhaps start a better conversation and elicit a chuckle or two;

- Are your welcome areas for visitors truly welcoming? Put up fun signs to welcome guests to your visitor parking, or add some fun to your welcome area with a humor bulletin board, funny signs, or some fun reading material. Include a guest book or photo album highlighting your workplace's accomplishments over the last year. Offer something for the kids or dogs. Provide a place where people are encouraged to sing your praises immediately on their favorite social media site;

- Hold a contest to solicit funny photos or videos from customers using your products or services in creative, offbeat ways;

- Offer unique services. The Westin Dublin offers a Digital Detox Package for guests, where they can safely leave all their electronic gadgetry behind for the duration of their stay and receive a Digital Detox survival kit;
- Offer an outrageous customer service guarantee. Zappos offers a full refund on any item for up to 365 days after the purchase, which is simply outrageous compared to most return policies. Or you can go the outrageously outrageous route and offer something funny: "Our service team will serenade you over the phone with a Celine Dion hit if you're not completely thrilled with our service;"
- A Vienna cafe offers sausages and special beer for dogs during the Munich beer festival. Some banks and retail businesses offer special places to tie dogs, with watering stations and doggie biscuits. Win over the dogs and chances are you win over their owners;
- Conversely, use some local pooches to warm the hearts of your customers. Fairmont Hotels throughout Canada have an official Canine Ambassador program. Each hotel has a dog in residence, all exceptionally well-behaved Labrador retrievers, who help greet guests and are available for guests to take for a walk;
- Offer something for your customers' kids, because there's a good chance that if you win over the kids, you win over the adults (and really, they're the ones with the serious buying power);
- Recognize loyal customers with offbeat awards and creative recognition. Reserve a parking space for them for the month, name a menu item after them for a month, honor the "customer of the month" with a fun photo on your wall, get your in-house choir together to sing a song of appreciation to them, honor them with a special "Customer of the Millennium" award;
- Celebrate local heroes in a fun way. Avalanche Movie Company, a movie-rental shop in Canmore, Alberta, changed the titles in its weekly newspaper listing of the top-ten movie rentals to fun alternative titles that recognized local heroes who helped deal with a natural disaster. Another Canmore

business, the Rocky Mountain Flatbread Company restaurant, created a Local Heroes display in their restaurant as a fun way to highlight community contributions;

- Celebrate offbeat or unusual theme days and holidays by posting them on a welcome board or by mentioning them on your voice mail;

- Link promotions to local events. A Victoria, BC restaurant changed its menu items to celebrate a concert by Elton John. The Boston Pizza chain of restaurants changed their name temporarily to Vancouver Pizza during the Stanley Cup hockey championships to show support for the Vancouver Canucks over their rivals for the cup, the Boston Bruins;

- Get your guests performing for you. Several hotels in California offered up a promotion wherein the first guest each day to sing a pre-selected song received a free room upgrade. The performances were videotaped and uploaded on YouTube and the hotels awarded a grand prize to the best performance of the summer;

- Create a fun customer loyalty oath or pledge. The Saskatchewan Roughriders, a football team in the Canadian Football League, generated copious amounts of publicity with a fun "Take the Riders' Oath" campaign;

- Create a fun greeting and/or departing ritual. Whenever a patron enters a Portland, Oregon bar everyone in the bar yells out a hearty "Yeah!" and when they leave, everyone boos. At Relish, a gourmet burger chain based in New Brunswick, Canada, employees yell a hearty "Hello!" every time a customer comes in. At AFA JCDecaux, clients arriving at their headquarters for important meetings are greeted by a team of enthusiastic employees in the parking lot, sometimes holding signs or wearing fun costumes;

- Create some offbeat amenities, something fun and unexpected, such as these offered up by various hotels:
    - A morning "run with the concierge" program—The Ottawa Westin;

- A 24-hour fragrance butler who arrives at your door with an array of colognes and perfumes—offered by some Rosewood Hotels;
- The Loews Coronado Bay resort in California offers a dog surfing instructor as part of its "Su'ruff Camp" for doggie guests;
- The Ritz-Carlton in Dallas, Texas has a "guacamologist" on hand, ready to help with any and all guacamole needs;
- New York's Benjamin Hotel has a sleep concierge, who helps you choose from an extensive array of pillows and sends up a peanut butter and jelly sandwich with warm milk if you are having trouble sleeping.

- Hire a celebrity impersonator or use local celebrities to "guest star" on your voice mail system messages;
- Create a section on your website where you display photos of your customers interacting with your business or products in a fun, creative way;
- Honor customers' heritage. The New Zealand B & B Te Puna Wai raises the flag of their guests' home nation in front of their house as a way to honor and welcome them;
- Break a rule to make it more fun for your customers. The Club Med resort in Turks and Caicos is an hour out of sync with the rest of the island for six months of the year: They don't observe Daylight Savings Time so they can give their guests an extra hour of daylight in the afternoon when they most want it;
- Use secret offers to make your customers feel like insiders. Many restaurants, for example, have "secret menu" items that aren't advertised on the menu. At the In 'n' Out burger chain, for example, you can order Animal-style Fries; at Starbucks you can order a Zebra Mocha. Many fancy-schmancy restaurants are also in on the secret menu club, offering unique options to diehard regulars in the know. Some advertise their secret menus on their websites; others claim, with a knowing wink, that the secret items don't actually exist;

- You don't have to be in the food biz to get in on the fun. Look for opportunities in your business to offer a secret special bonus to your long-time patrons. Start a rumor that lets customers know that when they say the secret word, order something at a certain time of day, or offer you the secret handshake, they'll get the key to your super-secret offer;

- Create a fun contest or promotion tied to natural events in your area. The Fairmont Chateau in Lake Louise, Alberta held a contest wherein guests had to guess the date their world-famous lake would thaw. You can tie promotions or contests to the first spring sighting of a robin, the first day in autumn when the leaves start changing, the first snowfall of the year, or even a lunar eclipse;

- "Kangaroos can't walk backward." This little bit of trivia I learned from a Snapples bottle cap. "The first American horse may have been a zebra." This I learned from the side of a U-Haul rental moving truck. Look for creative places to post fun facts and even better, make the fun facts relevant to your business;

- Create funny postcards of your team enjoying themselves at work and send them to your customers with a "Wish you were here!" greeting;

- Send out greeting cards at unusual times to celebrate minor and offbeat holidays and theme days such as Groundhog Day, Left-Handers' Day, or Hug an Australian Day;

As you might have guessed... I could go on and on. The key is to try something, *anything,* that includes your customers in the fun and makes them feel like an extended family member in your business. This is not limited to your customers, either. The more you make your vendors and suppliers feel like they are part of your extended family, the more dynamic your culture will become and the more your business will grow.

Exceed expectations.

Be different.

And laugh all the way to the bank.

## Key Messages and Ideas

1. To become known for your customer service, adopt a service-first attitude: "We are in the service business, we just happen to ______________."
2. Providing good customer service isn't good enough. Inspiring customer service occurs when you exceed expectations and do something differently than everyone else.
3. Great service matters and can become a central overriding value that leads to other benefits. Like poor service, memorable service can also go viral.
4. Happy customers create happy employees.
5. Humor might help reduce fee resistance when you're negotiating with customers.
6. Recognize and reward efforts for going the extra inch and the extra mile.
7. To instill a service sensibility throughout your culture, create a permanent visual reminder of the need for great service, communicate relentlessly, and recognize and reward great service.

# 10

# The Punch Line—Humor is No Joke

"Do not take life too seriously;
you will never get out of it alive."
– Elbert Hubbard

**S**o, does more funny really equal more money?

By now I've hopefully answered this question for you. This is important because making money is important. Businesses exist to turn a profit. Turning a profit allows your business to support families and communities.

But set aside the money factor for a moment and consider the idea that perhaps businesses also exist to make a difference: To lead change in the world we so desperately need, to model behaviors we want to see in the next generation and positively impact the lives of employees, employees' families, and customers. In the end, it's not just about making *you* richer, it's about making the lives of *everyone you touch* richer.

Ideally, business should be about putting people first, putting humanity first. Business should be about remembering that behind every anonymous customer and front-line employee lies a real person. And *that*, more than anything else, is what the humor advantage is all about—connecting at a more human level.

Humor is a connector, a builder, a catalyst. Humor shows us in our best light; it reminds us of our shared humanity and it has the power to transform experiences, ideas and people. Humor doesn't just have the potential to make us financially richer, humor makes our lives richer.

So once again here's the real bottom line that we started this journey with: Even if adding more fun and humor to your business doesn't help you achieve all the success I've suggested it might, what would you rather have: The same level of success and less fun, or the same level of success but a heck of a lot more fun along the way?

Start putting the humor advantage to work and maybe, just maybe, your entire life will become a little richer.

And *that* is money in the bank.

# Appendix A

## Five Ways to Jump-start a Culture Shift in Your Workplace

### 1. FOCUS ON THE IMPORTANT STUFF

Within less than a year the Denmark supermarket chain Irma transformed their culture (and saved their business) when a new CEO focused relentlessly on building a better culture. To achieve that goal the company focused on three areas: Leadership training based on personal development, open communication (including a very personal and heartfelt weekly newsletter that helped build trust and openness) and celebrating positive results. *Within less than a year* Irma became profitable and today is recognized as one of the best workplaces in Denmark and the best retailer to work for in Europe. *Focus on the key things that will give you the best bang for your time and energy.*

### 2. DO A VALUES BLITZ

AFA JCDecaux transformed their culture within four months by focusing intensely on one of their four core values for a week, cycling through a different value each week, repeating the process from the start until all four values became engrained into everyone's behaviors.

### 3. CREATE A THREE-IN-THREE CULTURE CHALLENGE

Challenge every employee *and every team* to do three things in the next three months to build a stronger, more inspiring culture.

## 4. USE A VCR APPROACH

**V**isual: Make it highly visual: Use signs, posters, badges, buttons, bumper stickers, mascots... whatever it takes to create a visual reminder of the desired changes or goals.

**C**ommunicate success stories on a consistent basis (open meetings with a "culture moment," or create a story section on your intranet).

**R**eward and recognize employees and teams who model the desired behavior.

## 5. MAKE THE PROCESS FUN

Being intentional about making the entire process of rejuvenating your culture fun and injecting more humor into your workplace will not only help you drive success, it also reflects a truly inspiring, successful culture.

# Appendix B

## Jump-starting More Fun at Work

### 1. CREATE A "FUN SQUAD" TO JUMP-START THE FUN REVOLUTION

To jump-start new initiatives to instill more fun at your workplace, create a dedicated team to take the initiative on implementing creative ideas. To show you're serious about this and to get the most dedicated people involved, don't just ask for volunteers, instead have people apply for a position on the fun squad.

Name the team something fun and inspiring, and make the entire process fun! Recognize and reward people for their ideas and input. Generate some buzz and excitement around the new team.

An alternative approach is to assign a "Corporate Jester" or "Director of Humor" in a rotating position of three or four months. This way, different people get rewarded with a chancc to do some fun and creative work and no one gets burned out doing it all themselves. The corporate jester can take the lead role organizing celebrations or initiating new fun rituals or office traditions.

Remember, though, creating a more fun workplace isn't the responsibility of a committee, a single person, or even just the leadership team, it's about permeating your entire culture with a spirit of fun energy. If you don't create a positive vision around the core values that people need to model, and create a culture of respect and appreciation, your efforts to increase the fun factor can be viewed cynically as band-aid solutions or window dressing.

### 2. MAKE FUN AT WORK A GOAL

If you're serious about fun at work, set some basic commitments. Spell out some specific targets for activities you're going to achieve within a given timeframe, such as, "Hold four social events in the next six months," or "Hold a fun awards ceremony by the end of June."

## 3. START A HUMOR RESOURCES LIBRARY

Start a humor-at-work library and stockpile it with humor books, articles and DVDs. The library can be used for employee orientation and training programs and serve as a source of information, ideas and inspiration for all employees.

## 4. MAKE IT VISIBLE

Create a collective team "humor first aid kit" full of funny books, photos, goofy props, funny costume parts, etc., that people can access when they need a good laugh. Spend a lunch hour cruising through a joke shop, costume store, party supply shop, or cruise the internet for ideas (websites such as "Trainers Warehouse" or clown supply catalogs offer great ideas).

## 5. START A HUMOR-AT-WORK FILE

Create a simple file or book where everyone can contribute their funny observations, funny articles, strange work-related trivia, statistics, or stories. This sends the message that your workplace values fun and that you want people to have fun. It also helps everyone grow their sense of humor by planting the seed in everyone's brain to be on the lookout for the funny stuff.

If you collect humor relevant to your profession or workplace, it will also be the most powerful kind of humor—insider humor, at which only you and your colleagues would laugh. *That's* the kind of humor that can create a sense of shared history and give your workplace a personality and a soul.

## 6. KEEP THE FUN-AT-WORK MESSAGE ALIVE

Remember, you do not create an inspiring workplace through a one- or five- or even ten-times-a-year event, and you don't create an inspiring workplace through things you can always check off on a 'to-do' list.

It's about *attitude.*

It's about the *simple* things everyone does on a *consistent* basis.

It's about reminding people that they have the power to choose their attitude and to choose to have a sense of humor about themselves and the things over which they have no control.

So keep the message alive:

- Set aside time to discuss this topic at your regular staff meetings;
- Create a fun-at-work bulletin board to remind people of the message;
- Create a workplace mascot that will serve as a constant visual reminder;
- Create simple daily, weekly or monthly traditions or rituals that serve to keep the message alive and kicking;
- Encourage your teammates to sign up to our free "Humor at Work" e-zine. The weekly e-zine offers a constant source of inspiration, fun and ideas. Sign up at www.HumoratWork.com.

## 7. GIVE PEOPLE PERMISSION TO HAVE MORE FUN

Give yourself and each other explicit permission to be more human, to have more fun, to play more and to bring a sense of humor along for the ride. Spread the enthusiasm. Share the laughter.

Nothing is more motivating than success and nothing is more *fun* than success!

# Appendix C

## Five Guiding Principles for Using Humor Effectively

### 1. FIRST, DO NO WRONG

Great advice for doctors or would-be corporate jesters. Make sure the humor you use laughs *with* people, not *at* people. Use humor to tear down walls, not to build new ones. Use humor that encourages creative thinking, not humor that squashes new ideas. Laugh at yourself, not in a, "I'm a loser" kind of way, but in a way that lets people know you don't take yourself overly seriously. Stay clear of political, ethnic, gender or sex-based humor.

Remember that having permission to use more humor at work is *not* permission to act like a jackass, a bore, or a jerk. It doesn't give you license to offend or humiliate people, or disparage their character.

It's about being more human, having a bigger heart and demonstrating greater humility.

### 2. BE AUTHENTIC

Humor can break down barriers and build trust, provided the humor creates and reflects authenticity. As Jerry Seinfeld once said, "The whole object of comedy is to be yourself. The closer to that you get, the funnier you will be."

This applies at a corporate level as well. Customers are savvier than ever and perhaps more cynical than ever. They'll see right through half-hearted attempts at humor that seem to be nothing more than manipulative and insincere window dressing.

## 3. BE CONGRUENT WITH YOUR BRAND

The humor you use at a corporate level must fit your style. It must be congruent with your brand. If you have a classy brand, your humor should be classy. If you want to be known as an edgy company, use edgy humor. Make sure the humor contributes to and reflects the brand image you want to project.

## 4. BE RELEVANT

The more the humor you use at your workplace is relevant to your business, the more memorable and effective it will be. Humor for the sake of humor can be a fabulous tool, but relevant humor that ties to your unique challenges, issues, products, local attractions and industry is far more impactful.

## 5. EMBRACE A SPIRIT OF FUN

It's more important to embrace a spirit of fun than it is to be funny. Embracing a spirit of fun suggests a lightness, a willingness to play and a spirit of inclusivity. A spirit of fun brings people together, motivates the troops and sparks creative thinking. It's about enjoying and celebrating the journey.

# What Next? What More?

## BRING THE HUMOR ADVANTAGE LIVE TO YOUR WORKPLACE OR CONFERENCE

Michael Kerr is one of Canada's most-requested speakers. His rave testimonials attest to the impact his presentations have on audiences around the world. *Nothing beats hearing the message first-hand.* Michael's outrageously energetic and hilarious presentations are known for their inspiring messages and for the tremendous amount of practical content jam-packed into each and every one—whether a short keynote speech or a full-day workshop with your leadership team.

To book Michael for your event contact Humor at Work at 866-609-2640 (US and Canada) or 01-403-609-2640, or drop us a line at info@mikekerr.com.

To download Michael's speaking kit (and for articles, videos and more resources), drop by the official Humor at Work website: www.HumoratWork.com.

## *THE HUMOR ADVANTAGE* BOOK FOR YOUR EVENT

What a fabulous idea! *The Humor Advantage* makes a great addition to your library and a fabulous thank-you gift for employees and clients. Ask us about bulk sale discounts for your team or company.

## WEEKLY HUMOR ADVANTAGE REMINDERS, IDEAS AND INSPIRATION

The key to building an inspiring workplace is forming habits and keeping the message alive. To help do just that we recommend that you and your team sign up for Mike's weekly e-newsletter, *Inspiring Workplaces—Humor at Work.*

It's a must-read for anyone serious about building a better workplace. At only one page it's a quick read, but it offers great inspiration and ideas on a range of topics, and it features Mike's fun-at-work tip of the week, a quote of the week, a look at the wacky side of life, and links to additional videos and articles. To sign up, drop by the home page at www.HumoratWork.com.

## THE THIRTY-DAY HUMOR ADVANTAGE VIDEO PROGRAM

Sign up for our 30-day program of daily, two-minute videos delivered right to your inbox. Each video offers a story, a message and a call to action designed to help you and your team foster a more inspiring workplace, all for less than the price of a cup of coffee a day. Team discount rates are also available so that everyone on your team receives the same daily dose of inspiration and ideas. For more details go to www.HumoratWork.com.

## RENT MIKE'S BRAIN

Bring Mike in to work with your team to help brainstorm ideas and facilitate an in-depth conversation about what your workplace needs to become a truly inspiring workplace that will attract and keep enthusiastic employees *and* customers.

Mike also offers one-on-one leadership coaching for leaders looking for ways to truly inspire their employees and make a serious difference in their lives and in their workplace.

## THE HUMOR ADVANTAGE CONTEST

Take photos of *The Humor Advantage* out and about in the world and post it to Instagram or Twitter with the hashtag #Humoradvantagebook or send a photo or video our way and you could win additional resources and prizes. The more fun, and the more creative, the better!

## BONUS RESOURCES ON THE WEBSITE

Bonus resources are available at the website www.thehumoradvantage.com. Enter the code "humor-me!" to gain access to a list of fun meeting openers, twenty ways to grow your sense of humor and the links to the videos referenced in the book. We'll add more bonuses over time, so be sure to drop back for a visit from time to time.

## ARE YOU LIVING THE HUMOR ADVANTAGE?

Mike continues to research inspiring leaders and workplaces around the globe, so if you think you have a message, story or company that people need to hear about, let us know.

# Endnotes


## FOREWORD

1. 2013 Gallup Poll on employee engagement, Gallup World website, http://www.gallup.com/poll/165269/worldwide-employees-engaged-work.aspx

## CHAPTER ONE

1. Interview with Paul Spiegelman, CEO Beryl Health, January 25, 2012.
2. "Muscles to Smile, Muscles to Frown," www.anatomynotes.ca, http://anatomynotes.blogspot.ca/2006/01/muscles-to-smile-muscles-to-frown.html
3. Fabio Sala, "Laughing All the Way to the Bank," *Harvard Business Review*, 2003.
4. R. Cronin, "Humor in the Workplace," Hodge-Cronin and Associates Survey, 1997.
5. Robert Half Survey: "Inside Joke: Humor Can Help the Bottom Line," Society for Human Resource Management, http://www.shrm.org/hrdisciplines/employeerelations/articles/pages/jokes-humor-workplace.aspx
6. Chris Robert, "Light Humor in the Workplace is a Good Thing," *University of Missouri New Bureau*, 2007.
7. "Bell Leadership Study Finds Humor Gives Leaders the Edge," Bell Leadership Study, www.bellleadership.com, 2012.
8. Robert F. Priest and Jordan E. Swain, "Humor and its Implications for Leadership Effectiveness," *International Journal of Humor Research*, Volume 15, Issue 2, June, 2002.
9. W.P. Hampes, "The Relationship Between Humor and Trust," *International Journal of Humor Research*, 12, 253-259, 1999.
10. Gil Greengross, Ph.D., "Are Women More Attracted to Men Who Court Them with Humor?" *Psychology Today*, 2011.

11. Courtney Rubin, "Why Happy Employees Are Good for Business," *Inc. Magazine*, 2010.
12. Alex Edmans, Lucius Li, Chendi Zhang, "Employee Satisfaction, Labor Market Flexibility, and Stock Returns Around The World," *National Bureau of Economic Research,* Wharton School of Business, July 2014.
13. Gretchen Rubin, *The Happiness Project,* HarperCollins Publishers Ltd., 2010.
14. Amy Lyman, "Trust, Friendships and Having Fun at Work," Great Places to Work Institute®, 2009.

## CHAPTER TWO

1. "Is Your Talent Pipeline at Risk? Engaging High Potentials," Human Capital Institute, 2011.
2. Interview with Jon Wolske, Zappos Insights, July 2012.
3. Mark Murphy, *Hiring for Attitude,* The McGraw-Hill Companies, 2011.
4. Shawn Achor, *The Happiness Advantage,* Crown Publishing Group, 2010.
5. Cary Cherniss, "The Business Case for Emotional Intelligence," Consortium for Research on Emotional Intelligence, 1999.
6. Kevin Freiberg and Jackie Freiberg, *Nuts! Southwest Airlines' Crazy Recipe for Business and Personal Success,* Bard Press, 1996.
7. Interview with Barry Williams, 2010.
8. Mercer Survey, reported in the *Globe and Mail Newspaper,* May, 2013.
9. Interview with Reid Carr, Red Door Interactive, 2012.
10. Personal communication, Lee Cockerell, February 2013.

## CHAPTER THREE

1. Dr. James Fowler study cited in "Emotions Are Contagious—Choose Your Company Wisely," *Psychology Today,* October, 2012.
2. Interview with Lara Morrow, January, 2012.
3. Jessica Pryce-Jones, *Happiness at Work - Maximizing Your Psychological Success at Work,* John Wiley and Sons, 2010.
4. James L. Heskett, *The Culture Cycle: How to Shape the Unseen Force that Transforms Performance,* FT Press, 2012.
5. Captain D. Michael Abrashoff, *It's Your Ship: Management Techniques from the Best Damn Ship in the Navy,* Business Plus, 2002.

6. Robert R. Provine, *Laughter - A Scientific Investigation,* The Penguin Group, 2000.
7. Owen Hanley Lynch, "Kitchen Antics: The Importance of Humor and Maintaining Professionalism at Work," *Journal of Applied Communication Research,* Vol. 37, No. 4, November, 2009.
8. "Fishy Business - Humor in a Sardinian Fish Market," *International Journal of Humor Research.* Volume 18, Issue 1, Pages 69–102, July, 2005.
9. Francesca Gino and Michael I. Norton, "Why Rituals Work," *Scientific America,* May, 2013.
10. Kareem J. Johnson and Barbara L. Fredrickson, "We All Look the Same to Me: Positive Emotions Eliminate the Own-race Bias in Face Recognition," *Association for Psychological Science,* University of Michigan, September, 2014.
11. Alison Wood Brooks, Juliana Schroeder, and Adam Waytz, "Understanding Rituals: Rituals' Effects on High-pressure Performance, Coping, Luck, and Consumption," *Academy of Management Proceedings,* January, 2013.
12. "Survey Shows How to Make Halloween a Scream in the Office by Glassdoor Team," 2013 http://employers.glassdoor.com/blog/survey-shows-how-to-make-halloween-a-scream-in-the-office/
13. Eileen Habelow, "Are Friendships the Key to Workplace Happiness?," *Forbes on-line,* April, 2010.
14. "New Research Reveals Job Satisfaction is Determined by Our Work Colleagues," Jobsite Website: http://www.jobsite.co.uk/insider/research-job-satisfaction-work-colleagues-10961/ October, 2012.
15. "The Collective Advantage," *Gallup Business Journal,* September 15, 2001.
16. Barbara Plester and Mark Orams, "Send in the Clowns: The Role of the Joker in Three New Zealand IT Companies," *International Journal of Humor Research.* Volume 21, Issue 3, Pages 253–281, September 2008.

## CHAPTER FOUR

1. Susan Ladika, "Companies Recognizing Importance of Recognition: Rewards & Recognition Providers," *Workforce Magazine,"* December, 2013.
2. "Engaging Gen X and Gen Y Employees: Three Significant Trends in Recognition," Achievers Whitepaper, www.achievers.com
3. Adrian Gostick and Chester Elton, *The Carrot Principle,* Free Press, 2007.
4. Dan Ariely, *Predictably Irrational: The Hidden Forces That Shape Our Decisions,* HarperCollins, 2008.

5. S.E. DeVoe and J. Pfeffer, "Time Is Tight: How Higher Economic Value of Time Increases Feelings of Time Pressure." *Journal of Applied Psychology*, January 17, 2011.
6. Gary Hamel, *The Future of Management*, Harvard Business School Publishing, 2007.
7. Teresa Amabile and Steven Kramer, *The Progress Principle: Using Small Wins to Ignite Joy, Engagement, and Creativity at Work,* Harvard Business Press, 2011.
8. Patrick Lencioni, *Three Signs of a Miserable Job*, John Wiley and Sons, 2010.
9. J. Richard Hackman and Greg R. Oldman, *Work Redesign,* Addison-Wesley Publishing Company, Inc., 1980.
10. Kate Rockwood, "Director of Homeland Happiness: How Kenexa is Blending Psychology and Technology to Create Passionate Workers," *Fast Company* magazine, November, 2008.
11. Carol S. Dweck, PhD, *Mindset: The New Psychology of Success,* Ballantine Press, 2006.
12. Po Bronson and Ashley Merryman, "The Praise Paradox," *National Education Association,* http://www.nea.org/home/42298.htm
13. Interview with Dr. Joseph Salley, CEO, Milliken and Company, December, 2012.
14. "Cows with Names Produce More Milk, Scientists Say," *The Telegraph,* January, 2009, http://www.telegraph.co.uk/earth/agriculture/farming/4358115/Cows-with-names-produce-more-milk-scientists-say.html
15. Amy Wrzesniewski, Clark McCauley, Paul Rozin, and Barry Schwartz, "Jobs, Careers, and Callings: People's Relations to Their Work," *Journal of Research in Personality*, 31, 21–33, Article No. RP972162, 1997.
16. Robert A. Emmons, *Thanks! How Practicing Gratitude Can Make You Happier,* Houghton Mifflin, 2007.
17. Robert A. Emmons and Michael E. McCullough, *The Psychology of Gratitude, Oxford University Press, Inc., 2004.* http://emmons.faculty.ucdavis.edu/
18. Nathaniel M. Lambert, "A Boost of Positive Affect: The Perks of Sharing Positive Experiences," *Journal of Social and Personal Relationships*, January, 2013.
19. Hal Rosenbluth, *The Customer Comes Second: Put Your People First and Watch 'em Kick Butt*, HarperCollins, 2002.
20. Presentation at National Speakers Association Convention by Dr. Marshall Goldsmith, August, 2008.

21. "Acts of Kindness Spread Surprisingly Easily: Just a Few People Can Make a Difference," *Science Daily,* March 2010. http://www.sciencedaily.com/releases/2010/03/100308151049.htm

## CHAPTER FIVE

1. Griffin M, "Open-door Policy, Closed-lip Reality," Corporate Executive Board, October, 2011.
2. Keith Ferrazzi, "Candor, Criticism, Teamwork," *Harvard Business Review*, January - February, 2012.
3. Brian Fugere, Chelsea Hardaway and Jon Warshawsky, *Why Business People Speak Like Idiots: A Bullfighter's Guide,* Free Press, 2005.
4. "What is the Losada Line? What is Meta Learning?," Losada Line Consulting, http://www.losadalineconsulting.net/#!losadaline/c5ro
5. Kathleen M. Eisenhardt, Jean L. Kahwajy, L. J. Bourgeois III, "How Management Teams Can Have a Good Fight: The Key Success Factors of the Most Performant Teams." *Harvard Business Review,* 1997.
6. Debra L. Roter, Judith A. Hall, *Doctors Talking With Patients/Patients Talking With Doctors,* Greenwood Publishing Group, 2006.
7. Margaret Heffernan, *Willful Blindness,* Anchor Canada, 2012.
8. Interview with Steve Cody, CEO Peppercomm, February, 2014.
9. Chip Heath and Dan Heath, *Made to Stick: Why Some Ideas Survive and Others Die,* Random House, 2007.
10. Dave Carroll, *United Breaks Guitars: The Power of One Voice in the Age of Social Media,* Hay House, Inc., 2012.
11. Russell Haley and Alan L. Baldinger, "The Use and Effect of Humor in Different Advertising Media," *Journal of Advertising Research,* 35, no 3 (1995) 44-56, 1997.
12. Fred K. Beard, *Humor in the Advertising Business,* Rowman and Littlefield Publishers, 2008.
13. Jim Lyttle, "The Effectiveness of Humor in Persuasion: The Case of Business Ethics Training," *Journal of General Psychology, 2001, 128 (2) 206-216, 2001.*
14. Thomas W. Cline, Moses B. Altsech, and James J. Kellaris, "When Does Humor Enhance or Inhibit Ad Responses?" *Journal of Advertising 32,* no. 3 (2003): 31-45, Fall, 2003.
15. Stephen Voltz and Fritz Grobe, *Viral Video Manifesto,* McGraw Hill, 2013.
16. Rebecca Burn-Callander, "UK Workers Waste a Year of Their Lives in Useless Meetings," *Management Today,* March, 2013.

## CHAPTER SIX

1. Edwin Catwull, *Creativity Inc.,* Random House Canada, 2014.
2. Matthew M. Hurley, Daniel C. Dennett, and Reginald B. Adams Jr., *Inside Jokes, Using Humor to Reverse Engineer the Mind,* MIT Press, 2011.
3. Jeff Dyer, Hal Gregerson, and Clayton M. Christensen, *The Innovator's DNA,* Harvard Business Review Press, 2011.
4. Leo Widrich, "Why We Have Our Best Ideas in the Shower: The Science of Creativity," Buffersocial, http://blog.bufferapp.com/why-we-have-our-best-ideas-in-the-shower-the-science-of-creativity.
5. Shelley Carson, *Your Creative Brain,* Harvard University, 2010.
6. Terry O'Reilly and Mike Tennant, *The Age of Persuasion,* Knopf Canada, 2010.
7. Jeffrey H. Dyer, Hal B. Gregersen, and Clayton M. Christensen, "The Innovator's DNA," *Harvard Business Review,* December, 2009.
8. L. Baroncelli, C. Braschi, M. Spolidoro, T. Begenisic, A. Sale and L. Maffei,"Nurturing Brain Plasticity: Impact of Environmental Enrichment," *Cell Death and Differentiation* 17, (2010) 1092–1103.
9. Ravi Mehta, Rui (Juliet) Zhu, and Amar Cheema, "Is Noise Always Bad? Exploring the Effects of Ambient Noise on Creative Cognition," *Journal of Consumer Research,* Vol. 39, No. 4 (December 2012), pp. 784-799.
10. Simone M. Ritter, Madelijn Strick, Maarten W. Bos, Rick B. Van Baaren, and Ap Disksterhuis, "Good Morning Creativity: Task Reactivation During Sleep Enhances Beneficial Effect of Sleep on Creative Performance," *Journal of Sleep Research,* Volume 21, Issue 6, 9 March, 2012.
11. Robert I. Sutton, *Weird Ideas That Work,* Free Press, 2002.
12. Charlan J. Nemeth, Bernard Personnaz, Marie Personnaz, and Jack A. Goncalo,"The Liberating Role of Conflict in Group Creativity: A Study in Two Countries," *European Journal of Social Psychology,* Eur. Journal of Social Psychology, 34, 365–374, 2004.
13. Leslie, Berlin, "We'll Fill This Space, but First a Nap," *New York Times,* September 2008, citing research by Harvard researcher Dr. Ellenbogen.
14. Daniel Kahneman, *Thinking, Fast and Slow,* Anchor Canada, 2011.
15. Amy Edmondson and James Detert, *"Latent Voice Episodes: The Situation-Specific Nature of Speaking Up at Work," Harvard Business School Working Paper Series,* no. 6-024, October 31, 2005.
16. Avner Ziv, "Using Humor to Develop Creative Thinking," *Journal of Children in Contemporary Society,* Volume 20, Issue 1-2, 1989.

17. Roger E. Beaty, Mathias Benedek, Robin W. Wilkins, Emanuel Jauk, Andreas Fink, Paul J. Silvia, Donald A. Hodges, Karl Koschutnig, Aljoscha C. Neubauer, "Creativity and the Default Network: A Functional Connectivity Analysis of the Creative Brain at Rest," *Neuropsychologia*, Volume 64, Pages 92–98, November 2014.
18. Isen, A.M. et al, "Positive Affect Facilitates Creative Problem Solving," *Journal of Personality and Social Psychology*, 52, 1122-1131, 1984.
19. Moshe Bar, "Use Your Delusion: A Neuroscientist on How Cheerful People Deceive Themselves," *Boston Globe Magazine*, 2014.
20. Teresa M. Amabile and Steven J. Kramer, "The Power of Small Wins," *Harvard Business Review*, May, 2011.
21. John Allman, *Evolving Brains,* Scientific American Library, W. H. Freeman, New York, 2000.
22. Tina Fey, Bo*ssypants,* Reagan Arthur Books, 2011.
23. Peter Sims, *Little Bets - How Breakthrough Ideas Emerge from Small Discoveries*, Free Press, 2011.

## CHAPTER SEVEN

1. Ed Mickolus, *The Secret Book of CIA Humor*, Pelican Publishing Group, 2011.
2. Judy Martin, "Stress at Work is Bunk for Business," *Forbes Magazine,* August 2, 2012. (Citing World Health Organization statistic of $300 billion annual cost to the US.)
3. "Workplace Stress Strains Organizations' Bottom Lines," *Corporate Wellness Magazine,* January 2014. http://www.corporatewellness-magazine.com/issue-24/worksite-wellness-issue-24/workplace-stress-strains-organizations-bottom-lines/
4. "Mental Health in the Workplace," *Workplace Resources for Employers,* Chrysalis stats cited. http://www.mentalhealthworks.ca/sites/default/files/free_resources/MHW_workplace_resource_web_June2012.pdf
5. Ruth Mantell, "How to Ease Your Workload," *Wall Street Journal*, April, 2011.
6. G. Johns, "Presenteeism in the Workplace: A Review and Research Agenda." *Journal of Organizational Behavior*, (2010): 31, 519-542.
7. Lakshmi Ramarajan, Sigal G. Barsade, "What Makes the Job Tough? The Influence of Organizational Respect on Burnout in the Human Services," Wharton School of Business, November 2006, http://d1c25a6gwz7q5e.cloudfront.net/papers/1327.pdf

8. Gretchen Spreitzer and Christine Porath, "Creating Sustainable Performance," *Harvard Business Review,* January-February 2012. http://hbr.org/2012/01/creating-sustainable-performance/ar/1

9. "Laughing Dog Sound Calms Shelter Dogs," www.examiner.com, July 2009.

10. "Give Your Body a Boost - With Laughter," WebMD, http://www.webmd.com/balance/features/give-your-body-boost-with-laughter

11. "Anticipating a Laugh Reduces Our Stress Hormones, Study Shows," *Science Daily,* April, 2008. http://www.sciencedaily.com/releases/2008/04/080407114617.htm

12. Rod A. Martin, *The Psychology of Humor - An Integrative Approach,* Elsevier Academic Press, 2007.

13. "School of Medicine Study Shows Laughter Helps Blood Vessels Function Better," University of Maryland Medical Center, March 2005. http://umm.edu/news-and-events/news-releases/2005/school-of-medicine-study-shows-laughter-helps-blood-vessels-function-better

14. M.G. Newman and A.A. Stone, "Does Humor Moderate the Effects of Experimentally-Induced Stress?," *Annals of Behavioral Medicine,* 18 (2) 101-109, June, 1996.

15. F. Strack, LL. Martin and S. Stepper S., "Inhibiting and Facilitating Conditions of the Human Smile: A Non-obtrusive Test of the Facial Feedback Hypothesis," *Journal of Personality and Social Psychology,* May, 1988; 54(5):768-77.

16. M. Iwase, Y. Ouchi, H. Okada, C. Yokoyama, S. Nobezawa, E. Yoshikawa, H. Tsukada, M. Takeda, K. Yamashita, M. Takeda, K. Yamaguti, H. Kuratsune, A. Shimizu, and Y. Watanabe, "Neural Substrates of Human Facial Expression of Pleasant Emotion Induced by Comic Films: A PET Study," *Neuroimage,* 2002 Oct 17(2):758-68.

17. C.C. Moran, "Short-Term Mood Change, Perceived Funniness, and the Effect of Humor Stimuli," *Behavioral Medicine,* 22(1), 32-38, 1996.

18. Julia Wilkins and Amy Janel Eisenbraun, "Summary of Laughter Benefits, Including Laughter vs. Treadmills and Seinfeld: Humor Theories and the Physiological Benefits of Laughter," www.academia.edu, 2009.

19. Paul McGhee, "Humor Reduces Job Stress," http://www.laughterremedy.com/article_pdfs/Stress.pdf

20. C.V. Ford and R. C. Spaulding, "The Pueblo Incident: A Comparison of Factors Related to Coping With Extreme Stress," *Archives of General Psychiatry,* 29(3), 340-343, 1973.

21. Adam Miklosi, Horvath, Zsuzsanna, Igyarto, and Botond-Zoltan, "Three Different Coping Styles in Police Dogs Exposed to a Short-term Challenge," *Hormones and Behavior,* 52(5), 621-630. December, 2007.

22. Brent A. Scott and Christopher M. Barnes, "A Multilevel Field Investigation of Emotional Labor, Affect, Work Withdrawal, and Gender," *Academy of Management Journal,* vol. 54 no. 1 116-136, February 1, 2011.

23. Howard J. Bennett, MD, "Humor in Medicine," *Southern Medical Journal,* 96(12), 2003.

24. Rod. A. Martin, *The Psychology of Humor - An Integrative Approach,* Elsevier Academic Press, 2007.

25. Herbert M. Lefcourt and Rod A. Martin, *Humor and Life Stress: Antidote to Adversity,* Springer-Verlag, 1986.

26. Rod. A. Martin, *The Psychology of Humor - An Integrative Approach,* Elsevier Academic Press, 2007.

27. Martin Seligman, *Learned Optimism,* Vintage Books, 2006.

28. Rose Hoare, "Barking Mad: Can Office Dogs Reduce Stress?," CNN, July 23, 2012. http://edition.cnn.com/2012/07/23/business/office-dogs-stress/

## CHAPTER NINE

1. "Companies Find It Pays To Be Nice to Employees," *Wall Street Journal,* July, 1998.

2. Karen O'Quin and Joel Aronoff, "Humor as a Technique of Social Influence," *Social Psychology Quarterly,* Vol. 44, No. 4, 349-357, 1981.

3. Paul McGhee, PhD, "Humor Boosts Sales," www.laughterremedy.com

4. Noah J. Goldstein, Robert B. Cialdini and Steven J. Martin, *Yes! 50 Scientifically Proven Ways to Be More Persuasive,* Free Press, 2008.

# Acknowledgements

Let's be clear: I know I am going to forget someone. Hopefully it's not you. If it is you, please forgive me and buy my book anyway.

As with my other five "babies," giving birth to this book was a labor of love. As an author friend of mine repeatedly warns me, "You have to be crazy to write a book these days. So you better be passionate about it."

What helped fuel my passion were the stories people told me of how inspired they were by their leaders, their workplaces and their mission in life. So my first heartfelt thanks goes out to all the people who so willingly agreed to free up their valuable time to tour me around their workplaces, who enthusiastically shared their stories or reviewed portions of the book, including...

Nicholas Brand, Men In Kilts; Mike Easton, Argus Industries; Paul Spiegelman, The Beryl Companies; Jon Wolske, Zappos; Lara Morrow, Beryl Health; Barry Williams; Jason Robinson and Janna Pantella, DIRTT Technologies; Reid Carr, Red Door Interactive; Alex Castley, Integris Credit Union; Michael Abrashoff; Kim Axelson, AFA JCDecaux; Kiki Nichols, Dawn Werry and Dr. Joseph Salley, Milliken and Company; Dr. Yoram Bauman; Steve Cody, Peppercomm; Dave Carroll, Beverly Brown and Ken Bland, SAS Institute Inc.; Dr. Rod A. Martin, University of Waterloo; Shaun Pozyn, Kulula Airlines.

A special thanks goes out to the talented and crazy Mike Vlessides, an extremely gifted writer and editor who offered suggestions, support, editorial guidance and encouragement throughout the project, copy editor Rod Chapman, and eagle-eyed, World Quiddler Champion Nancy Lewis for helping to take it across the finish line.

As always, a special thanks to Claudine Dumais—my #1 fan, my wife, my love, my friend and my business partner—for not only her editing prowess, but for her never-ending support, wisdom and cheerleading.

# Index

## D



## E



## F

## S



## T



## V

## W



## Y



## Z

# About the Author

(Or...as we say in Canada...aboot the author.)

Michael Kerr travels the world researching, writing and speaking about inspiring leaders and workplace cultures. He is recognized as one of North America's leading authorities on workplace culture and is listed as one of Canada's most in-demand speakers. In 2008, Michael became the 21st speaker to be inducted into the Canadian Speaking Hall of Fame.

Michael's ideas on building an inspiring workplace have been featured in *Fast Company, The Wall Street Journal, Forbes* on-line, *Alberta Venture* and the *Globe and Mail* newspaper. He is also a contributor to *Business Insider.*

Michael's other business books include, *You Can't Be Serious! Putting Humor to Work* and *Inspiring Workplaces*. He is also the author of *When Do You Let the Animals Out?, What's So Funny About Alberta?* and *The Canadian Rockies Guide to Wildlife Watching*.

Michael lives in Canmore, Alberta, in the spectacular Canadian Rockies.

Bring Michael to your next event (or to your workplace) to help *your* organization laugh all the way to the bank! Visit www.mikekerr.com or contact the world headquarters of *Humor at Work* at mike@mikekerr.com or 01-403-609-2640.